The Dynamics of Local Innovation Systems

This book offers a comprehensive overview of the dynamics underpinning the successful performance of local innovation systems (LIS), that is, spatial concentration of innovation activities in specific geographical areas, characterized by the synergetic co-localization of research centers, innovation-driven enterprises, large corporations and capital providers.

The reader will gain a deeper knowledge of LIS theory and learn about the theoretical and empirical challenges of studying the LIS from a relational perspective. The book also provides an analytical framework to explore the level of connectivity among LIS actors through the use of social network analysis (network architecture) and second, to assess the variety of different types of relationships that local actors put in place to produce innovation within the LIS (network portfolio). More specifically, this book explores which network configuration is associated with a successful LIS by deriving evidence from the empirical study of the biopharma LIS in the Greater Boston Area (GBA), which has been exemplified as a benchmark case in terms of successful LIS performance.

This book also contributes to the theoretical debate about the optimal configuration of network structure (e.g. network closure vs. network openness). In capturing the heterogeneous nature of the LIS demography, it addresses the challenges brought about by the adoption of a holistic approach. Finally, the study provides insights into the network portfolio composition, which has been underexplored by extant literature. Besides addressing the scientific community in the field, this book will also be a valuable resource with practical implications for policymakers and those actors willing to undertake an active role in the development of an LIS in their own regions.

Eva Panetti is a scholar in Innovation Management and Team Project Manager for the Massachusetts Institute of Technology's "Regional Entrepreneurship Acceleration Program" (MIT REAP) for the Campania Region (Italy). She gained her PhD in Management at the Federico II University of Naples and, since the beginning of her career, she focused her studies on the analysis of innovation ecosystems. In 2017 she was visiting researcher at the Massachusetts Institute of Technology's Industrial Performance Center, where she conducted a research project on Boston Biotech Ecosystem. She is the author of several international publications on innovation ecosystems, technology transfer and technological transitions. Having analyzed many international cases, her studies currently focus on the evolution of emerging innovation ecosystems, with special regard to the Industry–University relationship and technology transfer mechanisms, and are conducted in cooperation with the Department of Management and Quantitative Studies at the Parthenope University of Naples.

Routledge Studies in the Economics of Innovation

The Routledge Studies in the Economics of Innovation series is our home for comprehensive yet accessible texts on the current thinking in the field. These cutting-edge, upper-level scholarly studies and edited collections bring together robust theories from a wide range of individual disciplines and provide in-depth studies of existing and emerging approaches to innovation, and the implications of such for the global economy.

Automation, Innovation and Economic Crisis
Surviving the Fourth Industrial Revolution
Jon-Arild Johannessen

The Economic Philosophy of the Internet of Things
James Juniper

The Workplace of the Future
The Fourth Industrial Revolution, the Precariat and the Death of Hierarchies
Jon-Arild Johannessen

Economics of an Innovation System
Inside and Outside the Black Box
Tsutomu Harada

The Dynamics of Local Innovation Systems
Structures, Networks and Processes
Eva Panetti

For more information about this series, please visit: www.routledge.com/Routledge-Studies-in-the-Economics-of-Innovation/book-series/ECONINN

The Dynamics of Local Innovation Systems

Structures, Networks and Processes

Eva Panetti

LONDON AND NEW YORK

First published 2019
by Routledge
2 Park Square, Milton Park, Abingdon, Oxon OX14 4RN

and by Routledge
605 Third Avenue, New York, NY 10017

First issued in paperback 2020

Routledge is an imprint of the Taylor & Francis Group, an informa business

British Library Cataloguing-in-Publication Data
A catalogue record for this book is available from the British Library

Library of Congress Cataloging-in-Publication Data
A catalog record for this book has been requested

ISBN 13: 978-0-367-73021-5 (pbk)
ISBN 13: 978-0-367-19443-7 (hbk)
ISBN 13: 978-0-429-20239-1 (ebk)

Typeset in Bembo
by Apex CoVantage, LLC

Contents

Figures

Tables

Introduction

In recent decades we are witnessing a progressive spatial concentration of innovation activities in specific geographical areas characterized by a vibrant atmosphere due to the synergetic co-location of research centers, innovation-driven enterprises, large corporations and capital providers bound by horizontal and vertical relationships. In many cases, the physical proximity of a diverse community of actors engaged in innovation activities provides the context for new business formation, socio-economic regional growth and knowledge production at the global and local levels, with interesting implications in terms of co-evolutionary dynamics at the social, technological and environmental levels.

Scholars from both management and economic geography have labeled these environments local innovation systems (LIS) which, given their implications, have increasingly raised the interest of both academic and political communities. On the one hand, scholars from both management and economic geography have analyzed the conditions and criteria for LIS empirical recognition and judgment (i.e. system boundaries, actors and networks, institutions and knowledge dynamics) as well as the mechanisms for their creation in those regions presenting structural characteristics that may apparently prevent systems of innovation to emerge. On the other hand, institutional and government actors have been increasingly committed to policies to stimulate the emergence of dynamic innovation environments through, for example, the implementation of business accelerator programs, regimes of appropriability of intellectual property, tax incentives, the setup of incubators and co-working spaces and so forth. However, the mere co-location of innovation-oriented organizations and the establishment of incentives seem not to be sufficient conditions for LIS emergence. Indeed, as argued in the seminal work of Anna Lee Saxenian (1994), the successful performance of a system of innovation is largely due to the bottom-up emergence of synergetic cooperative mechanisms between organizations in the form of horizontal networks of relationships. In fact, relationships exert a key role for actors engaged in processes of innovation, as they enhance practices of inter-organizational cooperation that allow them to share risks related to new products, to accelerate their time to market, to bring together complementary skills and to gain access to financial resources and new technologies. Extant studies on innovation systems have started to analyze the network dimension as a further variable of LIS performance. However, analytical efforts toward the study of the LIS relational dimension have been limited and not fully explored. In particular, there seems to be a lack of agreement on the optimal configuration of network structure for the LIS assessment of performance. Additionally, most contributions tend to limit their analysis to inter-firm formal relationships, thus overlooking the heterogeneous nature of the system's components and the impact of looser ties. This book grounds on the recognition about the relevance of the relational dimension for the study of LIS as well as on the need to fill the gap in extant literature with respect to two aspects of analysis: network structure and network composition (i.e. the level of connectivity among the system's actors and the portfolio of different types of relationships and forms of cooperation that local actors put in place to produce innovation). While the first aspect relates to the debate as to whether a more open network is preferable than a more closed one, the second issues refers to the fact that, depending on circumstances, inter-organizational relationships may take the form of well-structured and long-term relations, as research and development (R&D) partnerships and joint ventures, as well as that of less formal interactions as in the case of know-how trading. More specifically, this book explores which configurations of network structure and portfolio are associated to a high-performing LIS by deriving evidence from the empirical study of the biopharma LIS in the Greater Boston Area (GBA), which has been exemplified as a benchmark case in terms of LIS successful performance. The empirical research adopts an explorative "critical" case study approach to derive propositions to orient future researchers, who are invited to test them and consider the results of this work as a benchmark for the study of LIS in emerging regions. Part of this research has been conducted at the Industrial Performance Center (IPC) of the Massachusetts Institute of Technology (MIT) under the supervision of Dr. Elisabeth Beck Reynolds. The IPC has constituted a privileged standpoint for the empirical observation of the biopharma LIS in GBA due to its location at the heart of Kendall Square, where major players of the industry are located, and due to the longstanding academic expertise of the IPC in the field of LIS. Additionally, the research design has been influenced by the MIT Innovation Ecosystem Framework that I assimilated at the MIT Sloan School of Management while attending the classes of the Regional Entrepreneurship Acceleration Laboratory (REAL), taught by Fiona Murray and Philip Budden, which have been fundamental for complementing the academic theoretical implications of the work with a more action-oriented approach.

The book is organized as follows. Chapter 1 provides a taxonomy of LIS definitions upon which an original and comprehensive definition of LIS is elaborated. The second part of the chapter offers an overview of the state of the art by classifying LIS studies in two main strands based on the identification of principal drivers of LIS performance (namely, the *input-driven* and the *output-driven* approaches) and positions the current work in one of them. Chapter 2 aims to explore a particular aspect that is studied within the *input-driven approach* (i.e. the relational dimension), which is the focus of the book.

To this purpose, the chapter provides an in-depth analysis of key concepts and empirical issues concerning this specific analytical perspective. More precisely, Section 2.1 discusses the key role played by networks of relationships within systems of innovation, with specific regard to the benefits deriving from partnering and the impact of network architecture on the access to relational capital. Section 2.2 provides an overview of the proximity framework, which highlights the conditions that favor network emergence. Section 2.3 introduces the use of social network analysis (SNA) as an approach for the study of LIS and illustrates the different positions within the debate on the desirable network structure to boost innovation system performance within network literature. Section 2.4 reviews empirical studies adopting an SNA approach for the study of LIS according to seven specific dimensions. Main findings emerging from the literature review lead to the identification of the literature gap, which is discussed in Section 2.5, before concluding. Chapter 3 illustrates and discusses the research strategy adopted for addressing the theoretical gap. Section 3.1 provides an overview of the exploratory case study methodology and emphasizes how the selected approach contributes to address the research questions. Section 3.2 provides an overview of the selected case study with particular regard to the relational implications of the drug development process, the identification of main players and the illustration and discussion of the typical forms of cooperation and interaction occurring between the industry players. A special section is dedicated to the illustration of the research techniques implemented for the empirical study highlighting their points of strength and limitations, the most common indicators and fields of application. Finally, Chapter 4 reports and discusses the main findings deriving from data analysis and develops an analytical framework for the study of the LIS relational dimension. More precisely, Section 4.1 provides snapshot metrics of the network structural configuration and identifies its central nodes. Section 4.2 discusses the results of direct interviews conducted with representatives of different organizations in the biopharma LIS in the GBA with the purpose of gaining insights about the preferable network portfolio combination along two dimensions: the impact on knowledge transfer and the importance of spatial proximity. Section 4.3 of the chapter provides an in-depth discussion of results from both analyses and combines them to achieve a more complete overview about the whole system's functioning and elaborates an analytical framework for future studies. Finally, a set of propositions for practitioners is presented in Section 4.4 together with main limitations of the study and suggestions for future research.

1 Local innovation systems

An overview

1.1 The impact of geography on innovation

Learning is considered as a key concept within innovation system literature. In the late 1980s, Lundvall (1985; Lundvall, Dosi, & Freeman, 1988) and Johnson (Johnson & Lundvall, 1994) introduced the notion of *learning by interacting* to emphasize the role of geographic proximity in providing a more direct and easy access to information within user-producer interactions (Lundvall, 1985). More specifically, the authors consider learning "a socially embedded process which cannot be understood without taking into consideration its institutional and cultural context" (Lundvall, 1992, p. 1). This is mainly explained by the fact that innovation generation represents a process characterized by low levels of predictability where learning plays a central role in such uncertain process, which in turn explains why complex and frequent communication between the parties involved is highly required, with specific regard to the exchange of tacit knowledge (Nonaka, Takeuchi, & Umemoto, 1996). The importance of geographic proximity in knowledge transfer processes is further emphasized with the introduction of the notion of *learning region* (Storper, 2005). In this regard, learning is conceived as a *territorially* and *socially* embedded and interactive process (Asheim, 1996), able to drive the successful growth and the innovation performance of regions (Cooke, 1992) thanks to the catalyst role of proximity (Coenen, Moodysson, & Asheim, 2004). Networking with other firms and organizations is therefore considered as a "learning capability" (Lundvall & Johnson, 1994), and different kinds of "learning relationships" (e.g. customer-supplier; cross-sectorial interactions) are deemed to be at the core of the innovation process (Johnson & Andersen, 2012).

Another important aspect is that the impact of geographic proximity on innovation-driven learning dynamics varies according to the nature of knowledge and innovation modes. Lundvall and Johnson (1994) grouped knowledge into four economically relevant knowledge categories:

- *Know-what*, i.e. knowledge about facts;
- *Know-why*, i.e. knowledge of scientific principles;
- *Know-who*, i.e. specific and selective social relations;
- *Know-how*, i.e. practical skills.

(p. 129)

This taxonomy is useful to understand the different channels through which learning takes place. Indeed, while *know-what* and *know-why* can be learned through codified information (e.g. by reading books or lectures), the other two forms of knowledge are more difficult to codify and may be required to be transferred through practical experience. Consequently, while *know-why* and *know-what* are more typically produced through STE-based innovation (science, technology and engineering), *know-how* and *know-who* are generally associated with DUI-based innovation (doing, using and interacting). Following Jensen, Johnson, Lorenz and Lundvall (2007), the STE mode is "based on the production and use of codified scientific and technical knowledge", whereas the DUI mode "relies on informal processes of learning and experience-based know-how" (p. 680). Main differences between the two modes of learning are shown in Table 1.1.

Asheim and Gertler (2005), building on the concept of learning as an interactive process, introduce a new dimension analytic dimension to the study of innovation processes (i.e. *knowledge base* Laestadius, 1998), which can be alternatively analytical or synthetic. The *analytical knowledge base* refers to industrial settings, "where scientific knowledge is highly important, and where knowledge creation is often based on formal models, codified science and rational processes" (Asheim and Gertler, 2005, p. 296), as in the case of biotechnology, information and communication technologies (ICT) and genetics. University-industry networks turn out to be particularly important, as companies tend to frequently rely on results from research institutions for the development of their innovations. The type of exchanged and produced knowledge tends to be codified, and its application gives origin to radical innovation

Table 1.1 STE mode vs. DUI mode

STE mode (science driven)	*DUI mode (user driven)*
Aim: Increase the R&D capacity of the actors in the system and increase cooperation between firms and R&D organizations	**Aim:** Foster inter-organizational learning and increase cooperation between in particular producers and users
Typical innovation policy:	**Typical innovation policy:**
Increase the R&D capacity of organizations	Support on-the-job learning and organizational innovations
Support joint R&D projects between firms and universities	Matchmaking activities and building and sustaining existing networks
Support higher education programs	Stimulate trust building and joint innovation projects between actors in the value chain (producers-suppliers, users-consumers)
Subsidies for R&D infrastructure (laboratories, research and technologies centers, research groups, etc.)	Stimulate joint projects between competing and auxiliary businesses
Support (financial) for increasing mobility between academia and industry	
Support for commercialization of research results	

Source: Isaksen and Nilsson (2011)

Table 1.2 Analytic vs. synthetic knowledge bases

Synthetic knowledge base	*Analytic knowledge base*
Innovation by application or novel combination of existing knowledge	Innovation by creation of new knowledge
Importance of applied, problem-related knowledge (engineering), often through inductive processes	Importance of scientific knowledge often based on deductive processes and formal models
Interactive learning with clients and suppliers	Research collaboration between firms (R&D department) and research organizations
Dominance of tacit knowledge due to more concrete know-how, craft and practical skill	Dominance of codified knowledge due to documentation in patents and publications
Mainly incremental innovation	More radical innovation

Source: Asheim and Gertler (2005)

more frequently. Indeed, radical innovation is typically produced when knowledge is exchanged among actors of different nature through inter-organizational relationships and cooperative mechanisms capable of stimulating reciprocal learning and thereby processes of innovation (Capaldo, 2004). Hence, the presence of actors of different nature (i.e. universities, firms, government institutions), presenting different skills and capabilities and diverse backgrounds can boost the creation of radical innovation as far as they exchange non-redundant information.

On the other hand, the *synthetic knowledge base* refers to "industrial settings, where the innovation takes place mainly through the application of existing knowledge" (Asheim and Gertler, 2005, p. 295) or through new combinations of knowledge. It is the case of incremental innovations, which are developed to solve specific problems as, for example, in the field of industrial machinery or shipbuilding, where products are generally manufactured on a small scale. Research and development (R&D) and university-industry links tend to be less important compared to the analytic knowledge base, and knowledge is often produced as a result of experimenting, testing and practical processes presenting a low level of codification. Main characteristics and differences of the two knowledge bases are summarized in Table 1.2.

The impact of spatial proximity on innovation processes thus manifests itself depending on the frequency and intensity of interactions (especially face-to-face) needed to effectively transfer the knowledge and the need of specific infrastructure (e.g. research institutions or innovation centers) for its development.

1.2 Defining a local innovation system (LIS)

1.2.1 A taxonomy of LIS definitions

Extant literature provides a variety of conceptual definitions of LIS (Table 1.3). Cooke, Uranga and Etxebarria (1998) and Doloreux (2002) emphasize embeddedness and learning mechanisms as key features of LIS. Indeed, while the

Table 1.3 Taxonomy of LIS definitions

Author (year)	*LIS definition*	*Focus*
Cooke et al. (1998)	A system "in which firms and other organizations are systematically engaged in interactive learning through an institutional milieu characterized by embeddedness"	Embeddedness
Asheim and Isaksen (1997)	LIS consists of a "production structure (techno-economic structures) and an institutional infrastructure (political-institutional structures)"	Role of policies and regulations
Tödtling and Kaufmann (1999)	LIS as a network inhabited by regional main industry's firms and by those operating in complementary fields whose relations are a vehicle for knowledge transfer and production	Inter-firm relationships
Doloreux (2002)	"Social system" where both private and public actors interact with each other in a systematic manner, thus contributing to the regional potential of the region concerned	Embeddedness
Morrison (2003)	LIS as "a set of localized network of actors (firms and organizations) devoted to generate, transform and diffuse knowledge"	Inter-organizational relationships; knowledge production and diffusion
Muscio (2006)	"Local innovation systems are based on the generation of regionalized learning systems where some local innovation policies are activated to transfer technologies, to enforce technological cooperation, and to provide support and incentives to innovative networks"	Role of policies; knowledge transfer
Norton (2007)	"LSI represents the collaboration and networks between companies and other players in the system (national and local government, regulatory authorities, research and training centers, the financial system and markets). It summarizes the diversity of roles of the various parts of the system – roles that are interlinked and interdependent"	Inter-organizational relationships
Canzanelli and Loffredo (2008)	"LIS are complex systems characterized by interaction between multiple actors and institutions that produce and reproduce knowledge and know-how, govern how they are transferred to businesses and other local organizations, and manage how they are implemented"	Inter-organizational relationships; knowledge production and diffusion
Hamaguchi (2008)	LIS as "as a subset of a cluster, differentiating from other kind of cluster by its very nature of orientation toward creation of products and production methods that are new to the industry"	Radical new knowledge production

(*Continued*)

Table 1.3 (Continued)

Author (year)	*LIS definition*	*Focus*
Russell et al. (2011)	"An innovation ecosystem refers to the inter-organizational, political, economic, environmental, and technological systems through which a milieu conducive to business growth is catalyzed, sustained, and supported. A dynamic innovation ecosystem is characterized by a continual realignment of synergistic relationships that promote growth of the system. In agile responsiveness to changing internal and external forces, knowledge, capital, and other vital resources flow through these relationships"	Interdependency of actors at multiple levels; inter-organizational relationships
Rahayu and Zulhamdani (2014)	"Local innovation system as an intelligent organism which has various organs with their unique tasks in order to achieve the main goal, i.e. innovation"	Interdependency of actors

Source: Author's own elaboration

former describes LIS in terms of a system "in which firms and other organizations are systematically engaged in interactive learning through an institutional milieu characterized by embeddedness" (Cooke et al., 1998, p. 1581), the latter refers to LIS as a "social system" where both private and public actors interact with each other in a systematic manner, thus contributing to the regional potential of the region concerned. The network argument is proposed also by Tödtling and Kaufmann (1999), who consider LIS a network inhabited by regional main industry's firms and by those operating in complementary fields whose relations are a vehicle for knowledge transfer and production. Similarly, according to Norton (2007):

> (LSI) represents the collaboration and networks between companies and other players in the system (national and local government, regulatory authorities, research and training centers, the financial system and markets). It summarizes the diversity of roles of the various parts of the system-roles that are interlinked and interdependent.
>
> (p. 13)

In this vein, Morrison (2003) defines LIS as "a set of localised network of actors (firms and organizations) devoted to generate, transform and diffuse knowledge" (p. 6) and, according to Canzanelli and Loffredo (2008), LIS are "complex systems characterized by interaction between multiple actors and institutions that produce and reproduce knowledge and know-how, govern how they are transferred to businesses and other local organizations, and manage how they are implemented" (p. 6). Other authors deepen the focus on relationships by emphasizing the interdependencies existing between local actors, as in the case of Rahayu and Zulhamdani (2014), who define "Local innovation system as an intelligent organism which has various organs with their unique tasks in order to achieve the main goal, the so called innovation" (p. 68). More specifically, these organs include: (1) operational organ (producers, local university, local research institute); (2) coordinator organ (business culture); (3) controller organ (business culture and the government); (4) planner/intelligence organ (the government); and (5) policy organ, or "brain" (the government). Asheim and Isaksen (1997) describe LIS as consisting of a "production structure (techno-economic structures) and an institutional infrastructure (political-institutional structures)" (p. 304). The catalytic role of institutions and local policies in stimulating the regional innovation performance is also stressed by Muscio (2006), who argues that "Local innovation systems are based on the generation of regionalized learning systems where some local innovation policies are activated to transfer technologies, to enforce technological cooperation, and to provide support and incentives to innovative networks" (p. 775). Hamaguchi (2008) provides an interesting contribution, emphasizing the innovation output as an LIS distinctive characteristic by defining it "as a subset of a cluster, differentiating from other kind of cluster by its very nature of orientation toward creation of products and production methods that are new to the industry" (p. 145), thus highlighting the specialization and the radical nature of the innovation produced within systems of this kind. A number of contributions have specified the elements or the required conditions for an LIS to exist. According to Gebauer, Nam and Parsche (2005), main LIS components include

> (i) horizontal and vertical relations among firms (e.g. prime contractors, subcontractors, independent enterprises in similar and/or different industries); (ii) firms' contacts with universities and other research institutions, as well as with technology centers; (iii) the role of government agencies (promotion), interest groups (commercial, technical and information support) and lending bodies (the provision of venture capital).
>
> (p. 662)

A more specific description of LIS main features is the one provided by Martin and Simmie (2008), that includes

> (i) Sectorally and institutionally diverse knowledge generating businesses and institutions which can draw innovative ideas from many potential sources; (ii) High levels of firm specialization to supply the best in national and international markets; (iii) Commercial and marketing know-how, based on knowledge of international market and technological conditions; (iv) a wider social culture that is also tolerant of diversity, and new ideas and ways of doing things; (v) Firms able to exploit knowledge and support knowledge applications by others; (vi) High levels of technical sophistication among both producers and users of technology; (vii) Economies of

> scale; (viii) International knowledge spillovers from sophisticated customers, including locally represented multinational companies, providing the local innovation system with information on leading edge knowledge, products and services.
>
> (p. 189)

A more recent study on the creation of LIS in emergent economies (Ferretti & Parmentola, 2015) identifies the following elements as critical for LIS creation: (1) a network of innovative firms, localized in the same area and bound by horizontal and vertical relationships; (2) a set of research and educational institutions, such as universities and research centers, which generate scientific knowledge that contributes to innovative processes; (3) a series of infrastructure provisions that incentivize the localization of innovative firms within the given area; and (4) the presence of cooperation mechanisms among all these actors, capable of stimulating reciprocal learning and thereby processes of innovation. Finally, from an ecosystem perspective (Russell, Still, Huhtamäki, Yu, & Rubens, 2011), "An innovation ecosystem refers to the inter-organizational, political, economic, environmental, and technological systems through which a milieu conducive to business growth is catalyzed, sustained, and supported" (p. 6) *and* that a dynamic innovation ecosystem is characterized by a continual realignment of synergistic relationships that promote growth of the system "in agile responsiveness to changing internal and external forces" (p. 7), and knowledge, capital and other vital resources flow through these relationships. The scholar identifies as actors of the innovation ecosystem (1) material resources (funds, equipment, facilities, etc.) and (2) human capital (students, faculty, staff, industry researchers, industry representatives, etc.) that in turn represents the (3) institutional entities (universities, colleges of engineering, business schools, business firms, venture capitalists [VC], industry-university research institutes, federal- or industrial-supported centers of excellence, and state and/or local economic development and business assistance organizations, funding agencies, policymakers, etc.).

1.2.2 The evolution of the study of LIS

The aforementioned concepts of knowledge base and embeddedness have been used as discriminatory criteria for distinguishing local innovation systems from other forms of territorial agglomerations (i.e. clusters; industrial districts and science and technology parks; Ferretti & Parmentola, 2015) (Figure 1.1). More specifically, LIS distinguish themselves by their high level of social embeddedness and the analytic knowledge base. The high level of social embeddedness stimulates and facilitates phenomena of *collective learning* or *learning through networking* and consequently, knowledge and information transfer. On the other hand, the existence of an analytic knowledge base suggests the co-location of firms and research and educational institutions as well as their close interaction within university-industry links.

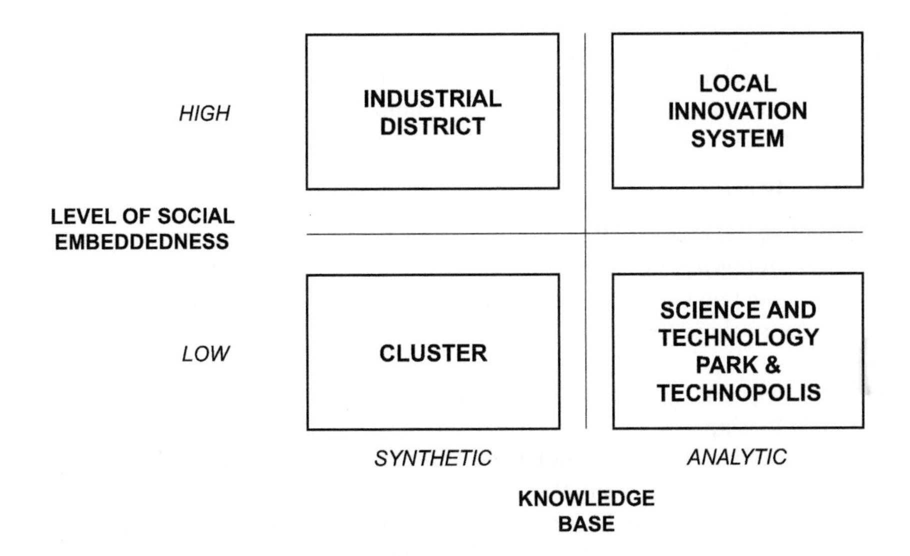

Figure 1.1 The dimensions of innovation systems

Source: Author's own elaboration from Ferretti & Parmentola (2015)

From the review of these contributions, a gradual shift from a more static toward a more dynamic conception of LIS emerges over time. More specifically, initial studies in the late 1990s appeared to be highly consistent with the literature arising around the learning region and the embeddedness, where regional institutions played a major role in stimulating those learning processes channeled by different types of proximity and trust mechanisms. Their focus was primarily on knowledge transfer as a driver for the performance of the single actors – mainly firms – and on the economic development of the region. In the early 2000s, the complexity of the system was made more evident by the conceptualization of the heterogeneity of LIS actors as a precondition not only for knowledge transfer but also for actual new knowledge production. As a consequence, the focus was not necessarily on the socio-economic development of the region hosting the LIS but rather on the performance of the LIS itself, and more particularly on its innovation output. Later on, with the introduction of the ecosystem perspective, the role of proximity as a catalyst for collective knowledge transfer was further emphasized as stimulating a community of interdependent actors. The focus shifted from the role of the heterogeneous actors' composition to that of inter-actor relationships (both at the individual and organizational levels), through which not only knowledge but also capital, technological capabilities and other vital resources for the system's growth are channeled. LIS was finally viewed as an intelligent organism where actors proactively respond to changing external and internal forces within a process of continuous and mutual realignment, where innovation is not the mere outcome of the system performance but rather a solution to those changes. Therefore, the system is not only seen as source of regional competitive advantage but also as a tool for technology transition toward more sustainable modes of production and consumption thanks to its ability to align visions and expectations of actors at multiple levels.

1.2.3 An extended definition of LIS

Grounding on extant literature, a local innovation system can be defined as a specific and promising geographic area characterized by a flourishing production of new knowledge as a result of the diffused adoption of open-innovation organizational modes and the presence of:

1. A network of innovative firms, bound by horizontal and vertical relationships;
2. A number of large corporations that establish a branch in the area and outsource part of their R&D activities;
3. A set of research and educational institutions (e.g. universities and research centers) which generate analytic base knowledge that contributes to innovative processes;
4. A number of initiatives and programs led by public institutions supporting knowledge exchange and innovation within the region;
5. A community of risk capital providers (e.g. venture capitalists, business angels) involved in activities of innovation scouting to diversify their portfolio of investments;
6. A series of infrastructures and facilities that incentivize the localization of innovative firms within the given area (e.g. incubator);
7. A great number of synergetic relationships among all these actors that promote the flow of knowledge, capital and other vital resources for the growth of the system.

The above definition of LIS refers to an ideal situation where the system is fully developed and grounds on the observation of benchmark cases of success where all the listed elements are in place (e.g. Silicon Valley or Kendall Square in Boston). From an evolutionary perspective, LIS may present all or some of the above elements according to their stage of development. Policies and programs supporting knowledge exchange and innovation within the region are generally key at the early stages of LIS development, especially in those emergent economies where it has been observed that government institutions usually undertake a leadership role in creating the LIS (Ferretti & Parmentola, 2015). On the other hand, the presence of a community of capital risk providers (e.g. venture capitalists, business angels) is usually typical of fully developed LIS in which the good performance of all other elements makes it appealing for investors to be located in the area. In other words, the physical proximity of risk capital providers may itself be seen as an indicator of the good performance of the system. Additionally, the presence of risk capital providers is strictly related to the regulatory system of the country hosting the LIS and the extent to which this does or does not incentivize private risky investments. However, the physical proximity of actors of different nature (industry, government and academia) bounded by a set of innovation-driven relationships seem to be the two basic conditions for the empirical recognition of LIS as such.

1.3 State of the art in LIS theory and classification of main studies

Extant literature tends to attribute the successful performance of systems of innovations to the heterogeneous composition of their actors or to their ability to produce new knowledge and to contribute to the regional economic growth. More specifically, existing contributions on the assessment of LIS performance can be divided in two broad groups. The first, which follows an *input-driven approach*, mainly focuses on the drivers of LIS performance, such as the actors' heterogeneous composition (e.g. Etzkowitz, 1996; Etzkowitz & Leydesdorff, 1995; Murray & Budden, 2017; Carayannis & Turner, 2006; Carayannis & Campbell, 2009; Carayannis & Campbell, 2012; Carayannis, Grigoroudis, & Goletsis, 2016); the spatial dimension (e.g. De la Mothe & Paquet, 1998; Cooke, 2001, 2004; Asheim & Coenen, 2005); the infrastructural endowment and policy incentives (e.g. R&D expenditure, venture investments, incubators and acceleration programs); and the relational dimension (e.g. Saxenian, 1994; Ahuja, 2000; Owen-Smith & Powell, 2004; Russell, Huhtamäki, Still, Rubens, & Basole, 2015), with specific regard to the creation of synergetic connections and cooperative mechanisms existing between the system's components. The second group, which follows an *output-driven approach*, privileges the focus on the effects of LIS creation in terms of production of new knowledge and contribution to the regional growth (e.g. Bajmócy, 2013; Campanella, Rosaria Della Peruta, & Del Giudice, 2014; Guan & Chen, 2010; Lerro & Schiuma, 2015). The following sections provide an overview of main perspectives within the two approaches.

1.3.1 LIS input-driven approach

This section reviews some of the main contributions appointing the successful performance of systems of innovations from a structural perspective. In particular, the reviewed studies tend to focus on three main structural elements of LIS: actors' heterogeneity, territorial boundaries and relationships. These input elements are considered preconditions of a successful LIS performance.

1.3.1.1 Actors' heterogeneity as a key performance indicator of LIS

The triple helix framework (Etzkowitz, 1996; Etzkowitz & Leydesdorff, 1995) has been traditionally employed within the literature of innovation systems as a valuable framework to explain the dynamics of complex systems in which knowledge production is the result of an interactive and heterogeneous

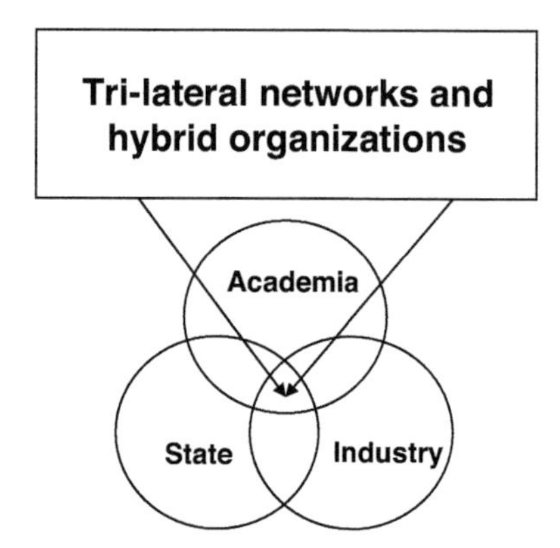

Figure 1.2 The triple helix model of university–industry–government relations
Source: Author's own elaboration from Etzkowitz (1996)

population of the network. The framework owes its popularity to the introduction of the industry–university–government (IUG) networks and the emphasis on the active role of public institutions carried out through a number of initiatives and programs supporting knowledge exchange and innovation within the region (Figure 1.2). In particular, the presence of government institutions in the network of innovative actors is particularly important as far as it is able to provide a series of infrastructure provisions that incentivize the localization of innovative firms within the area. Due to the potential for innovation deriving from the (non-redundant) transfer of information between different epistemic communities (researchers, managers, policymakers; Capaldo, 2004), the approach has found fertile ground within innovation system literature. Since its introduction, we are witnessing a proliferation of case studies committed to the evaluation of the system based on its actor base composition.

Extant studies not only focus on the physical co-location of the actors and their interactions but also on their engagement in the creation of the conditions that favor the emergence of LIS through their initiatives and activities. As a way of illustration, Braczyk, Cooke and Heidenreich (1998) propose a classification which distinguishes three typologies of LIS (grassroots, network and dirigiste) on the basis of their governance models and the implementation of technology transfer processes.

The *grassroots* model refers to an area where technology transfer is mainly developed and managed at the local level through the region's own organizations and government structures. In the *network* model, technology transfer results from the interplay of institutions at the local, national and global levels. Finally, in the *dirigiste* model, the technology transfer governance is mostly governed at the central level of national institutions. Ferretti and Parmentola (2015) provide an interesting framework for the classification of LIS (in the specific case of

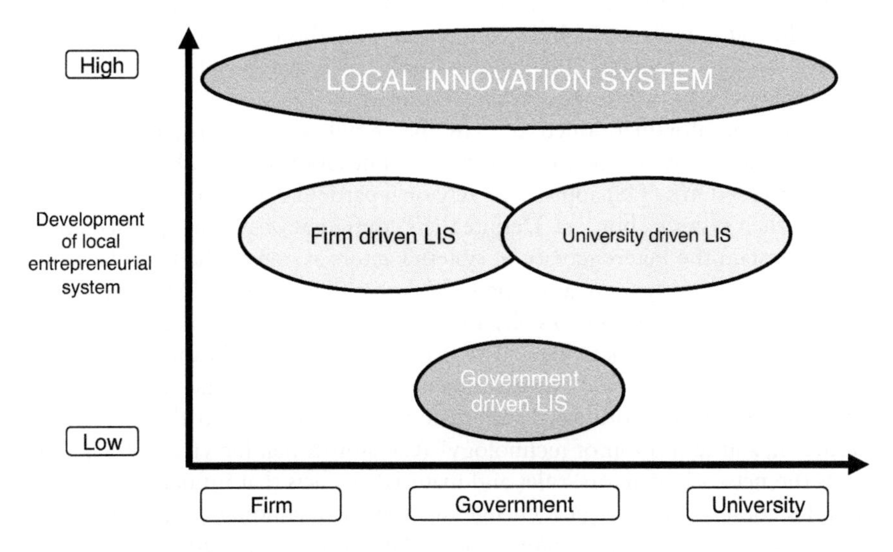

Figure 1.3 LIS classification based on the nature of the leading actor

Source: Ferretti and Parmentola (2015)

emergent nations), based on the typology of the actor who is taking a leading role in the process of LIS creation and the development level of local entrepreneurial system. More specifically, the creation of an LIS can be driven by one specific actor (a large company, a research institution or a local institution) that may take active role in enacting policies, setting the conditions to incentivize innovation in the local context or make it attractive for innovation firms' localization. The authors identify three typologies of LIS: (1) *government-driven* LIS, (2) *firm-driven* LIS and (3) *university-driven* LIS (Figure 1.3).

In this vein, another contribution (Ferretti, Panetti, Parmentola, & Risitano, 2017), while analyzing the development of a (port) innovation system in the City of Rotterdam (NH), focuses on the heterogeneous composition of the system with a high level of specialization of the (maritime) industry and provides insights on the *facilitator* role played by the Port of Rotterdam Authority (PORA). Due to PORA's mixed nature of *hybrid organization*, being engaged in both public and private domains with stronger performance requirements, the work presents interesting governance implications. Notably, the authors suggest that port authorities engage in cluster management by stimulating exchange of information and face-to-face interactions and by setting their own R&D program, as well as establishing joint ventures and other forms of cooperation with partners operating in the port's hinterlands. More recently, the importance of integrating the perspective of the media-based and culture-based public as well as that of embedding an ecology perspective has been emphasized as beneficial for knowledge-based development processes and policies. Both perspectives enlarged the traditional network composition of innovation systems and broadened the actor basis to include civil society (in the quadruple helix model; Carayannis & Campbell, 2009) and natural environments of society (in the quintuple helix model; Carayannis & Campbell, 2012).

Unlike the aforementioned systems that emphasize the spatial dimension of innovation activities, sectoral systems of innovation (SSI) and technological innovation systems (TIS) approaches rely on a particular sector or technology to delimit their systemic borders. Despite their configuration as non-spatial entities, they maintain the heterogeneity of system's actors as one of the main variables for the innovation systems' assessment. Malerba (2002) defines SSI as consisting of three main building blocks: (1) the knowledge and technological domain, (2) the actors and the networks and (3) institutions. On the other hand, a TIS is defined as "a network of agents interacting in the economic/industrial area under a particular institutional infrastructure and involved in the generation, diffusion, and utilization of technology" (Carlsson & Stankiewicz, 1995, p. 95), or as the network of actors, rules and material artifacts that influence the speed and direction of technological change in a specific technological area (Hekkert, Suurs, Negro, Kuhlmann, & Smits, 2007; Markard & Truffer, 2008). Finally, the recent contribution provided by the MIT Innovation Stakeholder Framework, besides recognizing the role played by IUG networks in systems of innovation, highlights the importance of the presence of a community of risk capital providers (e.g. venture capitalists, business angels) involved in activities of innovation scouting to diversify their portfolio of investments and providing the context for innovation-driven enterprises (IDE) to start, grow and scale (Murray & Budden, 2017). The developers of the MIT Innovation Stakeholder Framework identify five key groups of actors that play a crucial in the ecosystem: (1) entrepreneurs, (2) risk capital providers, (3) large corporations, (4) government and (5) universities. Ideally, these five actors should be working synergistically within the innovation ecosystem through collective action and cooperating to create the necessary conditions for supporting the growth of *innovation-driven enterprises* (IDEs). This specific kind of young firm differentiates from small and medium enterprises (SMEs) that need little start-up capital and lack of clear competitive advantage that, in turn, hinders their ability to grow quickly. Conversely, IDEs build on new ideas and technologies to generate rapid revenue and job growth after initial investment (Murray & Budden, 2017). Table 1.4 compares the reviewed studies based on the LIS actors that they consider.

1.3.1.2 *Territorial boundaries as a key performance indicator of LIS*

A number of approaches, especially from economic geography literature, have for a long time explored the optimal geographic configuration for the proper functioning of an LIS. Academic literature on LIS partly takes its roots from the traditional debate existing among the scholars of national innovation systems (NIS) (Freeman, 1989; Edquist, 1997) and regional innovation systems (RIS) (Cooke et al., 1998; Asheim & Gertler, 2005). Both perspectives share

Table 1.4 Actors' heterogeneity as a key performance indicator of LIS

Theoretical framework	*Author(s)*	*LIS actors*	*System's boundaries*	*LIS classification based on the actor's leading role*
The triple helix framework	Etzkowitz (1993) and Etzkowitz and Leydesdorff (1995)	Industry–university–government	Region	–
Local innovation systems	Braczyk et al. (1998	Industry–university–government	Region, nation and global	(1) Grassroots, (2) network and (3) dirigiste
Local innovation systems	Ferretti and Parmentola (2015)	Industry–university–government	Region	(1) Government-driven LIS, (2) firm-driven LIS and (3) university-driven LIS
Quadruple helix model	Carayannis and Campbell (2009)	Industry–university–government–civil society	Region	–
Quintuple helix model	Carayannis and Campbell (2012)	Industry–university–government–civil society–environment	Region	–
Sectoral systems of innovation (SSI)	Malerba (2002)	Industry–university–government	Technology	–
Technological innovation systems (TIS)	Carlsson and Stankiewicz (1991)	Industry–university–government	Industry	–
MIT Innovation Ecosystem Framework	Murray and Budden (2017)	Corporate–entrepreneurship–university–government–risk capital providers	Region	–

the belief that innovation originates from a network of institutions in the public and private sectors operating in the same territory. However, while the NIS approach identifies the optimal geographic context with the national boundaries, the latter confines innovation processes within the region from a meso-level perspective. In other words, while the RIS framework emphasizes the advantages for innovation activities deriving from the emergence of territorial industrial agglomeration, trust mechanisms and cultural proximity, the NIS perspective argues that innovation activities can be better stimulated through a coherent and cohesive set of regulations, policies and incentives at the country level. With specific regard to NIS, scholars emphasize four main components (Freeman, 1989): (1) the role of policy; (2) the role of corporate R&D in accumulating knowledge and developing advantages from it; (3) the role of human capital, the organization of work and the development of related capabilities; and (4) the role of industrial conglomerates in being able to profit from innovations emerging from developments along the entire industrial value chain standing upon three main "building blocks" (Lundvall, 1992): (1) sources of innovation (learning and search and exploration); (2) types of innovation (radical vs. incremental); and (3) non-market institutions (user-producer interactions and institutions) and set-up of actors (especially universities conducting R&D; Nelson, 1993). Finally, Soete (2012) recognizes the role of social capital (most importantly trust) in the interactive innovation processes. Scholars of geographic economy (Asheim, Isaksen, Nauwelaers, & Tödtling, 2003; Asheim & Gertler, 2005), starting from the assumption of the non-homogeneity within countries' regions (since many indicators can differ significantly in the areas of the same countries), developed a regionally based approach to innovation systems. Doloreux and Parto (2005) identify three main dimensions that characterize RIS: (1) the interactions between the actors of the innovation system in relation to the exchange of knowledge; (2) the setup and the role of institutions supporting knowledge exchange and innovation within a region; and (3) the role of RIS in regional innovation policymaking. In recent years, several scholars began to question the advantages of considering the region the fundamental geographic entity for describing the localized nature of innovation systems. Indeed, the LIS perspective, while recognizing the localized nature of innovation, differs from the previous approaches by maintaining the idea that innovation does not necessarily occur within the institutionalized geographic borders of a given area (Bunnell & Coe, 2001; Rantisi, 2002; Moulaert & Sekia, 2003) and may take different spatial configurations through the interplay of national, subnational and transnational systems. As a consequence, scholars started to use the term local innovation system to define a network of locally specialized and locally situated firms, institutions and research agencies that are involved in a process of collective learning, where this process is not limited within formal geographical borders (De la Mothe & Paquet, 1998; Cooke, 2001, 2004; Asheim & Coenen, 2005).

1.3.1.3 Relationships as a key performance indicator of LIS

Part of the studies approaching LIS from an analytical point of view emphasize the role of relationships between the different actors and organizations of the systems. Social *embeddedness* is one of the key concepts that is applied to the study of innovation systems to explain how non-market relations can favor mechanisms of trust, cooperation, collective learning or learning through interacting and discourage opportunistic behavior (Granovetter, 1985; Lyon, 2000). The concept of *embeddedness* is indeed useful to measure the level of cohesion and actors' integration in the LIS. In fact, high levels of cohesion can facilitate knowledge transfer mechanisms and consequently, LIS development. More specifically, relationships play a crucial role in LIS whether they generate practices of inter-organizational cooperation that allow actors, who are engaged in processes of innovation, to share risks related to new products and to accelerate their time to market as well as to bring together complementary skills and gain access to financial resources and new technologies (Kogut, 1989; Hagedoorn, 1993; Mowery & Teece, 1993; Eisenhardt & Schoonhoven, 1996; Chesbrough, 2003). As the case may be, relationships take different forms ranging from R&D strategic partnerships to joint ventures or to less structured forms of interaction, as in the case of co-organization of events or know-how trading (Uzzi, 1996). But primarily, relationships are a vehicle for new information or, in other words, source of informational advantage (Gulati, 1999), and scholars emphasize their potential for innovation in case of exchange of non-redundant information through ties between actors of different nature (Fagerberg, Martin, & Andersen, 2013). Adapted from the biological sciences, the ecosystem perspective contributes insights on the relational dimension of innovation. The term *innovation ecosystem* has been applied to address the complexities related to innovation (Durst & Poutanen, 2013) and the importance of relational capital (Still, Huhtamäki, Russell, & Rubens, 2014). Indeed, the innovation ecosystem perspective is based on the premise that communities consist of a heterogeneous and continuously evolving set of constituents that are interconnected through a complex global network of relationships. These constituents co-create value and are interdependent for survival (Moore, 1996; Iansiti & Levien, 2004; Basole & Rouse, 2008; Russell, Still, Huhtamäki, Yu, & Rubens, 2011; Russell et al., 2015; Basole, Clear, Hu, Mehrotra, & Stasko, 2013; Hwang & Horowitt, 2012; Mars et al., 2012). As argued by Jackson (2011), "an innovation ecosystem models the economic . . . dynamics of the complex relationships that are formed between actors or entities whose functional goal is to enable technology development and innovation" (p. 2). The author argues that the innovation ecosystem includes two different and largely separate economies: (1) the knowledge economy, driven by fundamental research and (2) the commercial economy, driven by the marketplace. Of necessity, indeed, the two economies are weakly coupled because the resources invested in the knowledge economy are derived from the commercial sector; this includes government R&D investments, which are ultimately derived from tax revenues. Inter-organizational relationships play a key role in connecting the two economies, especially when the actors involved have the ability to complement their skills for the creation of innovation production and commercialization, as for example the synergies existing between venture capitalists and young startups that go beyond exclusively investment relationships to include support and consultancy on business management issues.

When it comes to relations, there are at least two aspects to take into account. First, the nature and the characteristics of the ties that compose the network (i.e. the *network portfolio*) and second, the structural configuration of the network, with specific regard to its characteristics in terms of *closure* or *openness* and the average positions of nodes in terms of *centrality* or bridging function through structural holes (i.e. *network structure*). The seminal work of Saxenian (1994) represents a first attempt to relate the structure of networks to the performance of regional clusters: the more decentralized and horizontal industrial system of Silicon Valley seemed to outperform Route 128 which, conversely, was recognized as a network dominated by a few large firms with a high degree of vertical integration that privileges practices of secrecy and corporate hierarchies. A great part of contributions addressing the relational dimension for the evaluation of LIS originates from network literature. These contributions are reviewed in Chapter 2, leading to the identification of the literature gap that drives the formulation of the research questions and the realization of the empirical study.

1.3.2 LIS output-driven approach

While the *input-driven approach* tends to evaluate the innovation systems on the basis of their structural characteristics, the *output-driven approach* privileges the focus on the effects of LIS creation in terms of production of new knowledge (innovation output) and contribution to the regional growth from a functionalist perspective. Literature from different innovation systems' approaches provides a variety of alternative methods and indicators to measure innovation system performance. Based on a study conducted on 108 papers on innovation performance, Becheikh, Landry and Amara (2006) show that there is still a lack of agreement on which indicators better adapt to the measurement of innovation systems' performance (Figure 1.4). Some of the reasons behind this lack of common agreement can be traceable to:

- The *complex nature of innovation systems*, which makes it difficult to find a single indicator for measuring the multiple dimensions of the system in terms of actors, dynamics and impacts;
- The *lack of a commonly accepted definition of innovation itself.* More specifically, the selection of metrics depends on the type of innovation under analysis (radical vs. incremental or product vs. process);
- The *unclear distinction between innovation capacity and innovation performance* itself. In other words, the question is whether to focus on the number of innovations produced in a specific time frame or on the creation of environments and competencies capable of sustaining learning and innovation in the future.

Innovation involves multidimensional novelty (OECD, 1997), and therefore key problems with innovation indicators concern the underlying conceptualization of the object being measured, the meaning of the measurement concept and the general feasibility of different types of measurement. Edquist and Zabala (2009) clarify the difference between innovation capacity and innovation performance through the concepts of input and output. However, any indicator of both an input and output nature shows its limitations. Table 1.5 summarizes some of the main advantages and disadvantages of the most common used indicators.

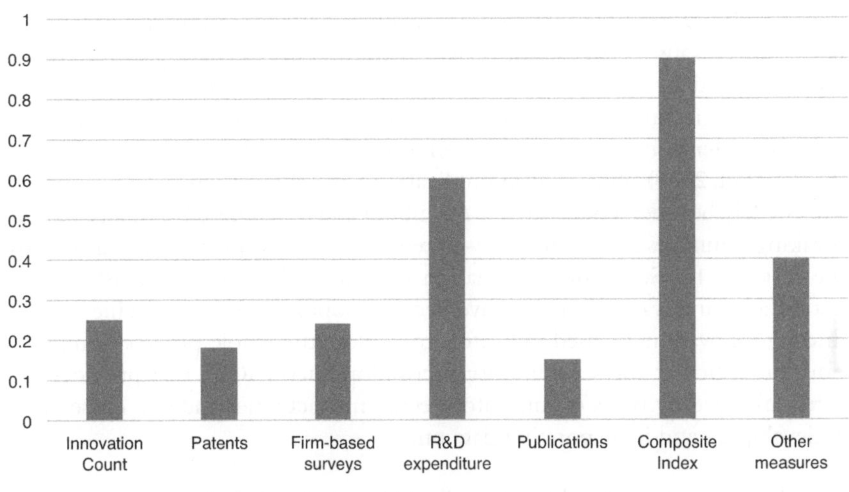

Figure 1.4 Most common innovation performance metrics

Source: Author's own elaboration from Becheikh et al. (2006)

Table 1.5 Most common used indicators of innovation performance

Indicator	*Advantages*	*Disadvantages*
R&D expenditure	Comparability time/countries	Overestimation of innovation; time lag not considered
Patents	Availability of detailed statistics; inventions are usually commercialized	Intermediate output indicator; time lag not considered
Innovation counts	Tangibility of innovation output	Favor radical innovation; favor product innovation
Scientific publications	Availability of detailed statistics	Favor English-speaking countries; quality can vary widely over countries
Royalties and license fees	Comparability time/countries	Acquisition of technology/ creation of technology

Source: Author's own elaboration

Current major indicators include input indicators such as R&D data (Archibugi & Coco, 2005), data on patent applications (Audretsch, 2004) and bibliometric data (citations and scientific publications). However, these metrics present some limitations, especially if these are used as single indicators. First, R&D data are considered to be indicators of innovation capacity rather than performance (Eggink, 2012), as well as being considered a measure that overestimates innovation (Audretsch, 2004; Becheikh et al., 2006; Greenhalgh & Rogers, 2010), as not all R&D expenditures do necessarily lead to innovation and conversely, not all inventions are the result of R&D investments. Second, patents, even if these are used in many studies as a measure of innovation output, are often considered "intermediate output" since these are deemed to measure *inventions* rather than *innovation*, and not all inventions are patented (Fagerberg & Srholec, 2009; LeBel, 2008). Finally, even publications are criticized, as their quality can vary widely between countries. As Archibugi and Coco (2005) noted, English-speaking countries risk being over-represented, as most journals monitored by the Institute for Scientific Information (ISI) are published in English. In the last decades, innovation surveys have become popular in order to achieve more directly innovation-focused indicators to explore the whole process of innovation. In particular, the Community Innovation Survey (CIS) that provides statistics analyzed by types of innovators, economic activities and size classes aims at developing and incorporating data on:

- Non-R&D inputs, such as expenditure on activities related to the innovation of new products (R&D, training, design, equipment acquisition, etc.);
- Outputs of incrementally and radically changed products, and sales flowing from these products;
- Sources of information relevant to innovation;
- Technological collaboration;
- Perception of obstacles to innovation, and factors promoting innovation.

(Fagerberg et al., 2005)

In order to overcome the problems of choice among input/output indicators, in the last 15 years there has been a proliferation of composite indicators, which became very popular within innovation systems literature. Indeed, scholars in the field, due to the systems' complex nature, tend to use composite indicators to overcome the possible problems related to the implementation of an incorrect or inaccurate single variable (Greenhalgh & Rogers, 2010). Some approaches tend to define innovation system performance in terms of functions achieved (Hekkert et al., 2007; Bergek, Jacobsson, Carlsson, Lindmark, & Rickne, 2008) and provide a set of indicators for each specific function (Hekkert et al., 2007). Carlsson, Jacobsson, Holmén and Rickne (2002), for example, measure innovation in terms of generation, diffusion and use of knowledge, displaying some possible measurements (Rickne, 2001) that may be combined for an effective evaluation of the system (Table 1.6). Other contributions define innovation system performance as the capacity of knowledge institutions to exploit the results of scientific research, thus providing quantitative data on patents, licensing, applied research projects and spin-offs (Acs, Anselin, & Varga, 2002; Fontes, 2005; Mustilli, Campanella, & Sorrentino, 2012).

There has been significant effort derived by international organizations that try to assess the innovative performance at the national and regional scales to inform political interventions, as in the case of the Revealed Regional System Innovation Index (RRSI; based on the European Innovation Scorecard

Table 1.6 Examples of performance metrics for an emerging technological system

Indicators of generation of knowledge	*Indicators of the diffusion of knowledge*	*Indicators of the use of knowledge*
Number of patents	Timing/the stage of development	Employment
Number of engineers or scientists	Regulatory acceptance	Turnover
Mobility of professionals	Number of partners/number of distribution licenses	Growth
Technological diversity (e.g. number of technological fields)		Financial assets

Source: Author's own elaboration from Rickne (2001)

Table 1.7 Composite indicators of innovation system performance

RRSI (Ue)	*ArCo Technology Index*	*Global Competitiveness Index (WEF)*
1. Population with tertiary education	1. Patents	1. Capacity to innovate
2. Participation in lifelong learning	2. Scientific articles	2. Quality of scientific research institutions
3. Employment in medium-high and high-tech manufacturing	3. Internet penetration	3. Company spending on R&D
4. Employment in high-tech services	4. Telephone penetration	4. University-industry research collaboration
5. Public R&D expenditure	5. Electricity consumption	5. Government procurement of advanced technology products
6. Business R&D expenditure	6. Tertiary, science and engineering enrollment	6. Availability of scientists and engineers
7. High-tech patent application	7. Mean years of schooling	7. Utility patents
	8. Literacy rate	8. Intellectual property protection

Source: Author's own elaboration from Bajmócy (2013)

[EIS]) or the Global Competitiveness Index (GCI), but also from innovation literature, as in the case of the ArCo Index developed by Archibugi and Coco (2004) that was constructed as the average of eight different indicators reflecting various aspects of technological capability (Table 1.7). These indexes combine both input (e.g. R&D expenditures) and output (e.g. patents and scientific publications) snapshot indicators to provide a picture of the system performance as complete as possible. An interesting contribution (Bajmócy, 2013) elaborates the Local Innovation Index, a functionalist approach, which assesses the system's performance based on 26 indicators (Table 1.8) that are

Table 1.8 The Local Innovation Index

Local Innovation Index			
F1. Knowledge creation (KC)	*F2. Knowledge exploitation (KE)*	*F3. Innovation background infrastructure (BI)*	*F4. Links (LINK)*
1. Government R&D expenditures (per capita)	1. Average number of valid home patent applications for four years (per capita)	1. # of newly registered enterprises (total number of enterprises)	1. # of patent co-applications as an average of four years (total number of co-applications)
2. Basic research expenditures (per capita)	2. Corporate R&D expenditures (per capita)	2. # of entries and exits (total number of enterprises)	2. # of microregions that have co-application links with the given micro-region as an average of four years
3. # of teaching staff in higher education institutions by location of headquarters (per capita)	3. Applied research expenditures (per capita)	3. # of population with maximum primary education subtracted from 100% (population aged 18–24)	3. # of majority or exclusively foreign-owned companies (per capita)
4. # of teaching staff in higher education institutions by place of education (per capita)	4. Experimental research expenditures (per capita)	4. # of employees with tertiary education (number of employees)	4. Net turnover of majority or exclusively foreign-owned companies (total number of companies)
5. # of graduating students (per capita)	5. # of enterprises at high- and medium-tech manufacturing (total number of enterprises)	5. # of inhabitants with tertiary education (population aged seven or above)	5. Total staff of majority or exclusively foreign-owned companies (total staff of companies)
6. # of students attending tertiary education (per capita)	6. Number of enterprises at high-tech Knowledge Intensive Business Services (total number of enterprises)	6. Number of ISDN lines (per capita)	6. Net turnover from export sales (total net turnover of companies)
	7. Number of full-time bachelor and master students (per capita)	7. Number of enterprises at Knowledge Intensive Market Services (total number of enterprises)	

Source: Author's own elaboration from Bajmócy (2013)

classified according to four functions (knowledge creation, knowledge exploitation, innovation background infrastructure and links).

1.4 Conclusions

This chapter provides a definition of LIS and offers an overview of the state of the art regarding the study of LIS performance. Based on the identification of the drivers of LIS successful performance, two main approaches are identified within the literature of innovation systems: the *input-driven approach* and the *output-driven approach*. Table 1.9 summarizes the main focal points of both streams. This work positions itself in the first stream of studies (the input-driven approach) and, more specifically, focuses on the relational dimension of LIS. This work provides a theoretical framework for the study of the relational dimension of LIS based on the assumption that the mere co-location of LIS actors per se does not necessarily identify an LIS as such (Russell, 2015) and that the bottom-up creation of synergies and cooperative mechanisms between local actors are the drivers for the proper functioning of an LIS given the advantages in terms of knowledge transfer, access to resources and pooling of complementary capabilities (Ahuja, 2000), thus contributing to both innovation creation and regional economic growth.

Table 1.9 LIS input-driven and output-driven approaches

Perspective	*Input-driven approach*		*Output-driven approach*	
	Structural		*Functional*	
Focus	Main actors' composition	Etzkowitz (1993), Etzkowitz and Leydesdorff (1995) and Murray and Budden (2017)	System innovation and economic output	Bajmócy (2013), Campanella et al. (2014), Guan and Chen (2010) and Lerro and Schiuma (2015)
	Spatial dimension	De la Mothe and Paquet (1998), Cooke (2001, 2004) andAsheim and Coenen (2005)		
	Relational dimension	Saxenian (1994), Ahuja (2000), Owen-Smith and Powell (2004) and Russell et al. (2015)		

Source: Author's own elaboration

References

Acs, Z. J., Anselin, L., & Varga, A. (2002). Patents and innovation counts as measures of regional production of new knowledge. *Research Policy, 31*(7), 1069–1085.

Ahuja, G. (2000). Collaboration networks, structural holes, and innovation: A longitudinal study. *Administrative Science Quarterly, 45*(3), 425–455.

Archibugi, D., & Coco, A. (2004). A new indicator of technological capabilities for developed and developing countries (ArCo). *World Development, 32*(4), 629–654.

Archibugi, D., & Coco, A. (2005). Measuring technological capabilities at the country level: A survey and a menu for choice. *Research Policy, 34*(2), 175–194.

Asheim, B. T. (1996). Industrial districts as "learning regions": A condition for prosperity. *European Planning Studies, 4*(4), 379–400.

Asheim, B. T., & Coenen, L. (2005). Knowledge bases and regional innovation systems: Comparing Nordic clusters. *Research Policy, 34*(8), 1173–1190.

Asheim, B. T., & Gertler, M. S. (2005). The geography of innovation: Regional innovation systems. In *The Oxford handbook of innovation*. Oxford: Oxford University Press.

Asheim, B. T., & Isaksen, A. (1997). Location, agglomeration and innovation: Towards regional innovation systems in Norway? *European Planning Studies, 5*(3), 299–330.

Asheim, B. T., Isaksen, A., Nauwelaers, C., & Tödtling, F. (Eds.). (2003). *Regional innovation policy for small and medium enterprises*. Cheltenham: Edward Elgar.

Audretsch, D. B. (2004). Sustaining innovation and growth: Public policy support for entrepreneurship. *Industry and Innovation, 11*(3), 167–191.

Bajmócy, Z. (2013). Constructing a local innovation index: Methodological challenges versus statistical data availability. *Applied Spatial Analysis and Policy, 6*(1), 69–84.

Basole, R. C., Clear, T., Hu, M., Mehrotra, H., & Stasko, J. (2013). Understanding interfirm relationships in business ecosystems with interactive visualization. *IEEE Transactions on Visualization and Computer Graphics, 19*(12), 2526–2535.

Basole, R. C., & Rouse, W. B. (2008). Complexity of service value networks: Conceptualization and empirical investigation. *IBM Systems Journal, 47*(1), 53–70.

Becheikh, N., Landry, R., & Amara, N. (2006). Lessons from innovation empirical studies in the manufacturing sector: A systematic review of the literature from 1993–2003. *Technovation, 26*(5), 644–664.

Bergek, A., Jacobsson, S., Carlsson, B., Lindmark, S., & Rickne, A. (2008). Analyzing the functional dynamics of technological innovation systems: A scheme of analysis. *Research Policy, 37*(3), 407–429.

Braczyk, H. J., Cooke, P., & Heidenreich, M. (1998). *Regional innovation systems: The role of governance in a globalized world*. London: Psychology Press.

Bunnell, T. G., & Coe, N. M. (2001). Spaces and scales of innovation. *Progress in Human Geography, 25*(4), 569–589.

Campanella, F., Rosaria Della Peruta, M., & Del Giudice, M. (2014). Creating conditions for innovative performance of science parks in Europe. How manage the intellectual capital for converting knowledge into organizational action. *Journal of Intellectual Capital, 15*(4), 576–596.

Canzanelli, G., & Loffredo, L. (2008). Territorial systems for innovation. *Evolution, 1*, 1.

Capaldo, A. (2004). *Strategia, reti di imprese e capacità relazionali*. Cedam.

Carayannis, E. G., & Campbell, D. F. (2009). "Mode 3" and "Quadruple Helix": Toward a 21st century fractal innovation ecosystem. *International Journal of Technology Management, 46*(3–4), 201–234.

Carayannis, E. G., & Campbell, D. F. (2012). Mode 3 knowledge production in quadruple helix innovation systems. In *Mode 3 Knowledge production in quadruple helix innovation systems* (pp. 1–63). New York: Springer.

Carayannis, E. G., Grigoroudis, E., & Goletsis, Y. (2016). A multilevel and multistage efficiency evaluation of innovation systems: A multiobjective DEA approach. *Expert Systems with Applications, 62*, 63–80.

Carayannis, E. G., & Turner, E. (2006). Innovation diffusion and technology acceptance: The case of PKI technology. *Technovation, 26*(7), 847–855.

Carlsson, B., Jacobsson, S., Holmén, M., & Rickne, A. (2002). Innovation systems: Analytical and methodological issues. *Research Policy, 31*(2), 233–245.

Carlsson, B., & Stankiewicz, R. (1991). On the nature, function and composition of technological systems. *Journal of Evolutionary Economics, 1*(2), 93–118.

Carlsson, B., and Stankiewicz, R. (1995). On the Nature, Function and Composition of Technological Systems, in Carlsson, B, (ed.) *Technological systems and economic performance: the case of factory automation*, Boston, Dordrecht and London, Kluwer Academic Publishers.

Chesbrough, H. (2003). *Open innovation: The new imperative for creating and profiting from technology*. Boston, MA: Harvard Business School Press.

Coenen, L., Moodysson, J., & Asheim, B. T. (2004). Nodes, networks and proximities: On the knowledge dynamics of the Medicon Valley biotech cluster. *European Planning Studies, 12*(7), 1003–1018.

Cooke, P. (1992). Regional innovation systems: Competitive regulation in the new Europe. *Geoforum, 23*(3), 365–382.

Cooke, P. (2001). Regional innovation systems, clusters, and the knowledge economy. *Industrial and Corporate Change, 10*(4), 945–974.

Cooke, P. (2004). The regional innovation system in Wales. In Regional Innovation Systems. *The Role of Governances in a Globalized World*, edited by Cooke, P., Heidenreich, M. and Braczyk, H., Routledge, 245–263

Cooke, P., Uranga, M. G., & Etxebarria, G. (1998). Regional systems of innovation: An evolutionary perspective. *Environment and Planning A, 30*(9), 1563–1584.

De la Mothe, J., & Paquet, G. (1998). Local and regional systems of innovation as learning socio-economies. *Economics of Science Technology and Innovation, 14*, 1–18.

Doloreux, D. (2002). What we should know about regional systems of innovation. *Technology in Society, 24*(3), 243–263.

Doloreux, D., & Parto, S. (2005). Regional innovation systems: Current discourse and unresolved issues. *Technology in Society, 27*(2), 133–153.

Durst, S., Poutanen, P. (2013). Success factors of innovation ecosystems: Initial insights from a literature review. *CO-CREATE 2013: The Boundary-Crossing Conference on Co-Design in Innovation*, Aalto University, 27–38.

Edquist, C. (1997). *Systems of innovation: Technologies, organisations and institutions*. London: Pinter.

Edquist, C., & Zabala, J. M. (2009). *Outputs of innovation systems: Accounting what comes out of the system*. Georgia Institute of Technology.

Eggink, M. E. (2012). Innovation system performance: How to address the measurement of a system's performance. *Journal of Innovation and Business Best Practices*, Article ID 593268, doi:10.5171/2012.593268.

Eisenhardt, K. M., & Schoonhoven, C. B. (1996). Resource-based view of strategic alliance formation: Strategic and social effects in entrepreneurial firms. *Organization Science*, 7(2), 136–150.

Etzkowitz, H. (1993). Technology transfer: The second academic revolution. *Technology Access Report, 6*(7).

Etzkowitz, H. (1996). From knowledge flows to the triple helix: The transformation of academic–industry relations in the USA. *Industry and Higher Education, 10*(6), 337–342.

Etzkowitz, H., & Leydesdorff, L. A. (1995). *Universities and the global knowledge economy: A triple helix of university-industry-government relations*. Retrieved from https://papers.ssrn.com/sol3/papers.cfm?abstract_id=2480085

Fagerberg, J., Martin, B. R., & Andersen, E. S. (Eds.). (2013). *Innovation studies: Evolution and future challenges*. Oxford: Oxford University Press.

Fagerberg, J., Mowery, D. C., & Nelson, R. R. (Eds.). (2005). *The Oxford handbook of innovation*. Oxford: Oxford University Press.

Fagerberg, J., & Srholec, M. (2009). Innovation systems, technology and development: Unpacking the relationships. In *Handbook of innovation systems and developing countries: Building domestic capabilities in a global setting* (pp. 83–115). Cheltenham: Edward Elgar.

Ferretti, M., Panetti, E., Parmentola, A., & Risitano, M. (2017). The port community system as a local innovation system: A theoretical framework. *Mercati & Competitività*, 2017(1), 97–118.

Ferretti, M., & Parmentola, A. (2015). Local innovation systems in emerging countries. In *The Creation of local innovation systems in emerging countries* (pp. 7–36). Springer International Publishing, New York City.

Fontes, M. (2005). Distant networking: The knowledge acquisition strategies of "out-cluster" biotechnology firms. *European Planning Studies, 13*(6), 899–920.

Freeman, C. (1989). *Technology policy and economic performance*. London: Pinter.

Gebauer, A., Nam, C. W., & Parsche, R. (2005). Regional technology policy and factors shaping local innovation networks in small German cities. *European Planning Studies, 13*(5), 661–683.

Granovetter, M. (1985). Economic action and social structure: The problem of embeddedness. *American Journal of Sociology, 91*(3), 481–510.

Greenhalgh, C., & Rogers, M. (2010). *Innovation, intellectual property, and economic growth*. Princeton, NJ: Princeton University Press.

Guan, J., & Chen, K. (2010). Measuring the innovation production process: A cross-region empirical study of China's high-tech innovations. *Technovation, 30*(5), 348–358.

Gulati, R., & Gargiulo, M. (1999). Where do interorganizational networks come from? *American Journal of Sociology, 104*(5), 1439–1493.

Hagedoorn, J. (1993). Understanding the rationale of strategic technology partnering: Interorganizational modes of cooperation and sectoral differences. *Strategic Management Journal, 14*(5), 371–385.

Hamaguchi (2008). *High-tech Brazil: Challenge of local innovation systems*. Retrieved from https://www.ide.go.jp/library/English/Publish/Download/Las/pdf/04.pdf

Hekkert, M. P., Suurs, R. A., Negro, S. O., Kuhlmann, S., & Smits, R. E. (2007). Functions of innovation systems: A new approach for analysing technological change. *Technological Forecasting and Social Change, 74*(4), 413–432.

Hwang, V. W., & Horowitt, G. (2012). *The rainforest: The secret to building the next Silicon Valley*. Los Altos Hills, CA: Regenwald.

Iansiti, M., & Levien, R. (2004). *The keystone advantage: What the new dynamics of business ecosystems mean for strategy, innovation, and sustainability*. Cambridge, MA: Harvard Business Press.

Isaksen, A., & Nilsson, M. (2011). Linking scientific and practical knowledge in innovation systems. *Papers in Innovation Studies 2011, 12*.

Jackson, D. J. (2011). What is an innovation ecosystem. *National Science Foundation, 1*.

Jensen, M. B., Johnson, B., Lorenz, E., & Lundvall, B. Å. (2007). Forms of knowledge and modes of innovation. *The Learning Economy and the Economics of Hope, 155*.

Johnson, B., & Andersen, A. D. (2012). *Learning, innovation and inclusive development: New perspectives on economic development strategy and development aid*. Aalborg Universitetsforlag.

Johnson, B., & Lundvall, B. A. (1994). The learning economy. *Journal of Industry Studies, 1*(2), 23–42.

Kogut, B. (1989). The stability of joint ventures: Reciprocity and competitive rivalry. *The Journal of Industrial Economics*, 183–198.

Laestadius, S. (1998). The relevance of science and technology indicators: The case of pulp and paper. *Research Policy, 27*(4), 385–395.

LeBel, P. (2008). The role of creative innovation in economic growth: Some international comparisons. *Journal of Asian Economics, 19*(4), 334–347.

Lerro, A., & Schiuma, G. (2015). Assessing performance and impact of the Technological Districts (TDs): General modelling and measurement system. *Measuring Business Excellence, 19*(3), 58–75.

Lundvall, B. Å. (1985). Product innovation and user-producer interaction. *The Learning Economy and the Economics of Hope, 19.*

Lundvall, B. A. (1992). *National systems of innovation: An analytical framework.* London: Pinter.

Lundvall, B. A., Dosi, G., & Freeman, C. (1988). Innovation as an interactive process: From user-producer interaction to the national system of innovation. In *Technical change and economic theory.* LEM Book Series from Laboratory of Economics and Management (LEM), Sant'Anna School of Advanced Studies, Pisa, Italy, (pp. 349–369).

Lundvall, B. A., & Johnson, B. (1994). The learning economy. *The Learning Economy and the Economics of Hope, 107.*

Lyon, F. (2000). Trust, networks and norms: The creation of social capital in agricultural economies in Ghana. *World Development, 28*(4), 663–681.

Malerba, F. (2002). Sectoral systems of innovation and production. *Research Policy, 31*(2), 247–264.

Markard, J., & Truffer, B. (2008). Technological innovation systems and the multi-level perspective: Towards an integrated framework. *Research Policy, 37*(4), 596–615.

Mars, R. B., Neubert, F. X., Noonan, M. P., Sallet, J., Toni, I., & Rushworth, M. F. (2012). On the relationship between the "default mode network" and the "social brain". *Frontiers in Human Neuroscience, 6*, 189.

Martin, R., & Simmie, J. (2008). Path dependence and local innovation systems in city-regions. *Innovation, 10*(2–3), 183–196.

Moore, B. (1996). *Sources of innovation, technology transfer and diffusion: The changing state of British enterprise.* ESRC Centre for Business Research, Cambridge.

Morrison, A. (2003). *Local systems of innovation in developing countries: Evidence from a Brazilian furniture cluster.* Università del Piemonte Orientale, Novara.

Moulaert, F., & Sekia, F. (2003). Territorial innovation models: A critical survey. *Regional Studies, 37*(3), 289–302.

Mowery, D. C., & Teece, D. J. (1993). Japan's growing capabilities in industrial technology: Implications for US managers and policymakers. *California Management Review, 35*(2), 9–34.

Murray, F., & Budden, P. (2017). *A systematic MIT approach for assessing "innovation-driven entrepreneurship".* ecosystems (iEcosystems).

Muscio, A. (2006). From regional innovation systems to local innovation systems: Evidence from Italian industrial districts. *European Planning Studies, 14*(6), 773–789.

Mustilli, M., Campanella, F., & Sorrentino, F. (2012). La valutazione delle performance innovative dei sistemi locali di innovazione: il caso dell'aerospazio e dei nuovi materiali in Campania. *Sinergie rivista di studi e ricerche, 84*, 209–229.

Nelson, R. (1993). *National systems of innovation: A comparative study.* New York: Oxford University Press.

Nonaka, L., Takeuchi, H., & Umemoto, K. (1996). A theory of organizational knowledge creation. *International Journal of Technology Management, 11*(7–8), 833–845.

Norton, M. G. (2007). Japan's eco-towns-industrial clusters or local innovation systems? In *Proceedings of the 51st Annual Meeting of the ISSS-2007* (Vol. 51, No. 2), Tokyo, Japan.

OECD. (1997). *National accounts, 1983–1995.* OECD.

Owen-Smith, J., & Powell, W. W. (2004). Knowledge networks as channels and conduits: The effects of spillovers in the Boston biotechnology community. *Organization Science, 15*(1), 5–21.

Rahayu, S., & Zulhamdani, M. (2014). Understanding local innovation system as an intelligent organism using the viable system model case study of palm oil industry in North Sumatra province. *Procedia-Social and Behavioral Sciences*, *115*, 68–78.

Rantisi, N. M. (2002). The local innovation system as a source of 'variety': Openness and adaptability in New York City's garment district. *Regional Studies*, *36*(6), 587–602.

Rickne, A. (2001). *Assessing the functionality of an innovation system*. Goteborg, Chalmers University of Technology.

Russell, M. G., Huhtamäki, J., Still, K., Rubens, N., & Basole, R. C. (2015). Relational capital for shared vision in innovation ecosystems. *Triple Helix*, *2*(1), 1–36.

Russell, M. G., Still, K., Huhtamäki, J., Yu, C., & Rubens, N. (2011). Transforming innovation ecosystems through shared vision and network orchestration. In *Triple Helix IX International Conference*, Stanford, CA, USA.

Saxenian, A. (1994). *Regional networks: Industrial adaptation in Silicon Valley and route 128*. Cambridge, MA: Harvard University Press.

Soete, L. (2012). *Maastricht reflections on innovation: Tans lecture 2011*. Retreived from https://www.merit.unu.edu/publications/working-papers/abstract/?id=4639

Still, K., Huhtamäki, J., Russell, M. G., & Rubens, N. (2014). Insights for orchestrating innovation ecosystems: The case of EIT ICT Labs and data-driven network visualisations. *International Journal of Technology Management*, *66*(2–3), 243–265.

Storper, M. (2005). Society, community, and economic development. *Studies in Comparative International Development (SCID)*, *39*(4), 30–57.

Tödtling, F., & Kaufmann, A. (1999). Innovation systems in regions of Europe: A comparative perspective. *European Planning Studies*, 7(6), 699–717.

Uzzi, B. (1996). The sources and consequences of embeddedness for the economic performance of organizations: The network effect. *American Sociological Review*, 674–698.

2 Local innovation systems as networks of relationships

2.1 The impact of network architecture in innovation processes

2.1.1 Innovation networks: key concepts

Networks of innovating firms are identified in different configurations: supplier-user networks, networks of pioneers and adopters, regional inter-industrial networks, international strategic technological alliances and professional inter-organizational networks (DeBresson & Amesse, 1991). According to economic sociology, whether operationalized in informal ties among individuals (Granovetter, 1985; Uzzi, 1996), interlocking affiliations among corporations (Mizruchi, 1992; Davis, Yoo, & Baker, 2003) or formal, contract-based strategic alliances (Eisenhardt & Schoonhoven, 1996; Powell, Koput, & Smith-Doerr, 1996), networks represent a key component of markets due to their ability to channel and orient flows of information and resources within a social structure. Innovation literature generally appoints networks as critical to innovation process with specific regard to knowledge-intensive sectors, where innovation involves the transformation of the results of scientific results into marketable products and services.

2.1.2 Benefiting from innovation networks

Depending on the choices about the preferred mode of commercialization, firms may decide to operate only in the upstream phases of the value chain, thus focusing on production and then selling their intellectual property, or rather opt for a full or partial engagement in downstream operations by developing and selling their products directly to the market (Arora, 2002). In both cases, relationships with external organizations play a crucial role but, depending on a firm's location in the value chain, they assume different forms ranging from licensing agreements and venture investments for the development of the technology (as in the first case) to strategic alliances for gaining access to the market for product commercialization. In particular, young small firms operating in knowledge-intensive industries, such as biotechnology or software development, are those that are more likely to benefit the most from networking, with specific regard to (1) reputation advantages, (2) access to information and (3) resource mobilization.

1 *Reputation advantages.* Primarily, social networks play a particularly important function during the early stages of business formation and development as they provide *credibility and legitimacy* to young business, thus decreasing the high level of uncertainty and risk perception related to technologies that have not yet proven their efficacy on the market (Moensted, 2007).
2 *Access to information.* Second, networks are a vehicle for new information or, in other words, source of *informational advantage* (Gulati, 1999), especially about the quality and location of resources. Network literature emphasizes their potential for innovation in the case of exchange of non-redundant information through ties between actors of different nature (Fagerberg, Martin, & Andersen, 2013).
3 *Resource mobilization.* Finally, networks can be exploited for *mobilizing the resources* required during the innovation process (Stuart & Sorenson, 2003). Actors operating in knowledge-intensive industries may require both technological and non-technological resources. While the former highly depend on the knowledge base that prevails in the industry and are generally channeled through research and development (R&D) projects, science and technology (S&T) partnerships, patents (both in co-development and provision practices) and non-technological resources generally refer to *complementary assets* (Teece, 1986) that are required to commercialize and capture value from the technology, as in the case of financial capital, manufacturing or marketing services, regulatory knowledge and so forth.

2.1.3 Why network structure matters: the impact of network architecture on resource mobilization

Access to resources through social networks has been the object of analysis of both literature on social networks and entrepreneurship as well as literature on innovation networks. The former considers that entrepreneurial activities are essentially social processes that are *embedded* in networks of social relationships among individuals (Aldrich, Zimmer, & Jones, 1986; Uzzi, 1997) which, in combination with the social environment, highly affect business formation and development (Huang, Lai, & Lo, 2012). On the other hand, literature on innovation networks emphasizes the role of networks in giving access to *critical resources* (especially technological and scientific knowledge) in alternative or in combination to the market (Ozman, 2009), which make them key during the early stages of business formation and development.

However, resource mobilization through networks may vary according to specific dimensions of network architecture. Salavisa, Sousa and Fontes

(2012) identify four aspects affecting the process of resource access, namely, network size, network composition, network positioning and relational structure.

As far as *network size* is concerned, following Burt (2000), the larger the network, the more complete and diverse is the set of available resources, and entrepreneurs can use indirect ties to enlarge their personal network and gain access to a larger quantity of assets. With regard to *network composition*, there is a traditional debate whether main advantages can be traceable to the concepts of *heterophily* and *homophily*. On the one hand, scholars emphasize the benefits of actors' diversity in terms of non-redundant exchange of knowledge and information (Burt, 2002; Nooteboom, 1999; Baum, Calabrese, & Silverman, 2000). On the other hand, a network homogenous composition can make solid and long-term partnerships more likely and enhance mechanisms of trust and collective problem solving (Powell et al., 1996). As for *network positioning*, a position of centrality in the network has been considered to give advantages in terms of new partnership formation (Ahuja, 2000; Gulati & Gargiulo, 1999), access to key resources and business economic and innovation performance (Powell, Koput, Smith-Doerr, & Owen-Smith, 1999). Finally, *relational structure* is a concept relative to the nature of ties (strong vs. weak, formal vs. informal, simple vs. multiplex) that the network's actors choose to establish with their partners in order to gain resources. Contrasting visions characterize the debate on which relational structure ensures a better performance and main arguments relate to the trade-off existing between the potential for innovation deriving from weak and informal ties and the trust-based exchange of information resulting from strong ones. The long-standing debate on the optimal network structure will be analyzed in depth in the next sections.

2.2 The proximity framework

2.2.1 The role of proximity in the emergence of knowledge networks

The role of proximity in favoring practices of knowledge transfer and the emergence of inter-organizational relationships has increasingly gained the attention of scholars from organizational and management studies (Oerlemans & Meeus, 2005; Knoben & Oerlemans, 2006; Ritter & Gemünden, 2003; Molina-Morales, García-Villaverde, & Parra-Requena, 2014; Molina-Morales, Belso-Martínez, Más-Verdú, & Martínez-Cháfer, 2015; Presutti, Boari, & Majocchi, 2013) and from regional and urban studies (Kirat & Lung, 1999; Huber, 2012). In economic geography, the issue concerning the positive relationships between geographic proximity and tie formation has for a long time been one of the most debated questions (Morgan, 2004). The intuitive positive association between spatial distance and tie formation has been empirically validated by a number of studies (e.g. Bell & Zaheer, 2007; Maggioni, Nosvelli, & Uberti, 2007; Abramovsky & Simpson, 2011). However, other forms of proximities have also been proven to act as substitute of geographic concentration in stimulating network formation (see e.g. Singh, 2005; Agrawal, Cockburn, & McHale, 2006; Sorenson, Rivkin, & Fleming, 2006; Ponds, Van Oort, & Frenken, 2007; Breschi, Lenzi, Lissoni, & Vezzulli, 2010). A stream of studies within evolutionary economic geography has provided a significant contribution to this field of research through the elaboration of an analytic framework (the *proximity framework*) that extends the notion of proximity to multiple dimensions and allows isolating geographical proximity as only one of the potential factors stimulating the emergence of networks. Originating from the French school of proximity dynamics (Gilly & Torre, 2000; Torre & Rallet, 2005; Carrincazeaux, Grossetti, & Talbot, 2008), which represents the first attempt to combine geographical proximity with other forms of similarities (i.e. the organizational proximity), the *proximity framework* owes its popularity to the work of Boschma (2005) that analyzes the relationship existing between proximity and innovation. The author starts from the assumption that "geographical proximity cannot be assessed in isolation" and that "geographical proximity per se is neither a necessary nor a sufficient condition for learning to take place" (p. 61). Boschma proposes a framework that combines five dimensions of proximity (cognitive, organizational, social, institutional and geographical proximity), which are deemed to positively influence the emergence of knowledge networks. The underlying idea is that practices of inter-organizational cooperation are more likely to occur if the parties show certain similarities. In other words, the involved actors should present a certain level of *homophily* (McPherson, Smith-Lovin, & Cook, 2001) not necessarily limited to the spatial co-location. The next few sections discuss each of the forms of proximity included in the framework.

2.2.2 Geographical proximity

In its simplest form, the term refers to the physical distance that separates two organizations and their economic activities (Gilly & Torre, 2000) and that is deemed to enhance face-to-face interactions. More recently, scholars have distinguished co-location and geographical proximity with the aim to specify that actors can share geographic proximity even without being co-located by the means of the so-called *temporary geographic proximity* (Torre, 2008) that allows two organizations to interact through visits, meetings and conferences. Traditionally, geographical propinquity has been considered as a source of competitive advantage in the literature of agglomeration economies (Rosenthal & Strange, 2001), technological clusters (Porter, 1998) and Italian districts (Becattini, Bellandi, & De Propris, 2014). Beyond material factors, such as the reduction of transport and logistics costs or access for the use of common technological platforms, spatial proximity has also been deemed as a condition enhancing the particular transfer of tacit knowledge, a key driver of innovation processes and its stickiness (Bathelt, Malmberg, & Maskell, 2004) in networks of local systems of innovation (Audretsch & Feldman, 1996; Howells, 2002; Tallman, Jenkins, Henry, & Pinch, 2004).

2.2.3 Cognitive proximity

This dimension of proximity refers to the conditions of similitude that facilitate the emergence of ties among actors sharing common knowledge bases and competences (Nooteboom, 2000; Knoben & Oerlemans, 2006). More specifically, this particular kind of proximity is deemed to drive the so-called *absorptive capacity* (Cohen & Levinthal, 1990) within interactive learning processes among the parties involved in the relationships. However, organizations cooperate in order to gain access to external and new knowledge, which in turn requires a certain degree of cognitive distance between the involved parties. As a consequence, this leads to a trade-off between the novelty of the exchanged information (deriving from different knowledge bases) and the efficacy of communication (resulting from similar knowledge background Balland, 2012). Consequently, cognitive proximity is considered as one of the key decisions driving the choice of future partners.

2.2.4 Organizational proximity

This category of proximity indicates that actors belonging to the same organization or to the same *corporate group* and show a greater tendency to share knowledge and innovate. More precisely, this organizational proximity refers to "the level of strategic interdependence among two organizations, which reduces uncertainty about the behavior of the future partner" (Balland, 2012, p. 744). This proximity occurs between partners belonging to the same organization, that is, between parent companies and subsidiaries. According to Boschma (2005), the degree of organizational proximity depends on the extent of autonomy and control induced by their tie. More specifically, actors sharing a high level of organizational proximity tend to avoid more easily unintended knowledge spillovers and decrease the uncertainty rate, which in turn leads to a reduction in the costs of collaboration "by providing an easier exchange of engineers, working groups or meetings" (Balland, 2012, p. 744) as well as a more available exchange of relevant information about the knowledge bases of the involved parties, with good results in terms of efficacy of the collaboration and cognitive matching (Balland, 2012).

2.2.5 Institutional proximity

Following Edquist and Johnson (1997), institutions are defined as a "set of common habits, routines, established practices, rules, or laws that regulate the relations and interactions between individuals and groups" (p. 46). Consequently, a distinction can be made between formal institutions (e.g. laws and rules) and informal institutions (as habits and cultural norms) that, according to Boschma, implies both the idea of economic agents sharing a common language, law system, regulations and language that provide the basis for coordinating and collective action. This type of proximity is therefore considered to reduce uncertainty and transaction costs. Therefore, institutional proximity can be regarded as an enabling factor that provides the stability required for interactive learning to take place. On the other hand, institutional proximity may also be a source of local inertia when the restructuring of old and rigid structures meets resistance from conservative actors who see change as a threat to their vested interests, leaving no space for "experiments with new institutions that are required for the successful implementation of new ideas and innovations" (Boschma, 2005, p. 68).

2.2.6 Social proximity

The idea of social proximity is generally expressed through the concept of *embeddedness* (Polanyi, 1944; Granovetter, 1973) and emphasizes the crucial role played by individual and personal ties (the *old boys' network*) in establishing economic relationships on the basis of trust mechanisms. Balland (2012) shows that actors are more inclined to form ties with individuals that share their same behaviors in relational dynamics. More precisely, social proximity refers to reputation and trust effects resulting from experience achieved through past collaborations and repeated interaction among the actors over time. Personal relationships, friendships and mostly trust enhance the transfer of informal communication that induces organizations with a common partner to cooperate with each other.

To sum up, organizations are more likely to cooperate with each other when they present similar knowledge bases; belong to the same corporate group; share common norms, values and routines; are embedded in a common social context; or are co-located in the same geographical region (Balland, 2012). According to the proximity framework, geographic proximity may ease interactive learning but does not represent a sufficient condition or a necessary one. More precisely, spatial propinquity is not necessary because it can be replaceable by other types of proximity to address the problems of coordination, and it is not sufficient because learning processes need a certain extent of cognitive proximity to be efficient. However, besides stimulating tie formation, all different forms of proximity also play a role in increasing the effectiveness of knowledge transfer and novelty generation.

2.2.7 The risks of "too much proximity"

The advantages of proximity in terms of more efficacy in communication, discouragement of opportunistic behavior and limitation of unintended local knowledge spillovers have been widely discussed in the literature and have found common agreement. However, it is argued that an environment with organizations in excessive proximity can be detrimental as far as proximity shapes a condition of *knowledge overload* (Granovetter, 1973) as a result of an excessive network "closeness" that can be harmful for new knowledge generation and can prevent learning from taking place (Geldes, Felzensztein, Turkina, & Durand, 2015). This phenomenon has also been referred to as the "proximity paradox" (Broekel & Boschma, 2011; Cassi & Plunket, 2014) and depicts a condition of too much proximity. Such a condition is considered to cause some undesired effects that may hinder innovation from taking place (Boschma,

2005), with particular regard to *lock-in mechanisms* deriving from a too-closed network or local inertia as a result of extremely rigid institutions that are resistant to change, as well as a lack of sources of novelty due to redundancy of information between agents and organizations sharing a common knowledge base and high level of cognitive proximity. A significant number of empirical contributions demonstrate how excessive cognitive proximity could eventually reduce inter-organizational knowledge exchange, and a too-high level of closeness between partners on any proximity dimension could be harmful for their innovation performance. As a way of illustration, Ben Lataifa and Rabeau (2013) investigate the reasons and the mechanisms through which proximity may impede the creation of new entrepreneurship. In this vein, Molina-Morales et al. (2015) explore the potential negative effects resulting from the diverse forms of proximity and show that the existence of cognitive and institutional proximities negatively affect link generation in the firm's later stages. In order to meet some of these inconveniences, Boschma (2005) proposes a set of adjusting mechanisms that can be traceable to the achievement of a knowledge base consisting of a diverse yet complementary set of capabilities; the constitution of more loosely coupled networks; the combination of both embedded and market relations between agents; a mixed innovation system model between *local buzz* and opening to extra-territorial linkages; and a common institutional system that guarantees checks and balances (Table 2.1). Moreover, the role of geographical proximity has been the object of further criticism by a stream of studies that emphasizes the *virtualization* of inter-firm relationships – as a result

Table 2.1 The proximity framework

	Key dimension	*Too little proximity*	*Too much proximity*	*Possible solutions*
1. Cognitive	Knowledge gap	Misunderstanding	Lack of sources of novelty	Common knowledge base with diverse but complementary capabilities
2. Organizational	Control	Opportunism	Bureaucracy	Loosely coupled system
3. Social	Trust (based on social relations)	Opportunism	No economic rationale	Mixture of market and embedded relations
4. Institutional	Trust (based on common institutions)	Opportunism	Lock-in and inertia	Institutional check and balances
5. Geographical	Distance	No spatial externalities	Lack of geographical openness	Mix of local "buzz" and extra local linkages

Source: Author's own elaboration from Boschma (2005)

of globalization – and downsizes the role of spatial concentration in network development (Fitjar, Huber, & Rodríguez-Pose, 2016).

2.3 The social network approach for the study of innovation systems

Social network analysis (SNA) has been widely implemented for the sociological study of individuals and organizations (Wasserman & Faust, 1994; Welser, Gleave, Fisher, & Smith, 2007) as well as for the assessment of nested structures of inter-firm relationships (Moody & White, 2003; Halinen, 2012). In particular, studies within economic geography have paid increasing attention to relational issues (Dicken, Kelly, Olds, & Wai-Chung Yeung, 2001; Bathelt & Glückler, 2003; Yeung, 2005) and provided a rich narrative on spatial dynamics of evolution. However, despite their valuable contribution, these studies have been the object of criticism by a number of scholars who appoint the lack of formalization and scientific rigor as one of the main weaknesses of this approach (see e.g. Giuliani & Bell, 2005; Cantner & Graf, 2006; Grabher, 2006; Glückler, 2007; Sunley, 2008). Balland, De Vaan and Boschma (2012) argue that these flaws in relational approach can be partially overcome through the use of network analysis, as it "allows for a quantitative investigation of inter-organizational interactions" (p. 743). More specifically, networks' main components are actors (nodes) and their relationships (edges), and visual network analysis can serve as a tool for revealing the flow of information, know-how and financial resources among different actors (Russell, Still, Huhtamäki, Yu, & Rubens, 2011). Relational metrics can allow for a deeper understanding of a system's emergent structures, patterns and transformation dynamics (Freeman, 2002) as well as for a comparative analysis over time and across regions. As a result, scholars in economic geography have increasingly adopted network analysis within their methodology choices (Murdoch, 2000; Grabher & Ibert, 2006; Bergman, 2009; Ter Wal & Boschma, 2009) with specific regard to the study of certain endogenous structural network effects (Glückler, 2007) such as *transitivity* or *preferential attachment* mechanisms in driving network evolution. More precisely, while the former refers to the so-called *triadic closure* – that is, the tendency of two unconnected nodes to tie with each other in case they share a common partner (Davis, 1970; Holland & Leinhardt, 1971) – the latter refers to the attractiveness exerted by nodes in a position of high centrality within the network that leads new entering nodes to partner with them (Barabási & Albert, 1999) (Figure 2.1). Apart from the drivers of network evolution, many scholars have increasingly focused on the effects and implications of structural characteristics of networks on the knowledge transfer and innovation performance. Contrasting visions have characterized this specific stream of studies, which is illustrated in the next section.

2.3.1 The debate on the desirable network structure: key concepts

Network literature is traditionally characterized by two contrasting visions about the desirable structure of networks, namely Coleman's *network closure* and Burt's *structural hole* arguments. The debate is about the identification of which

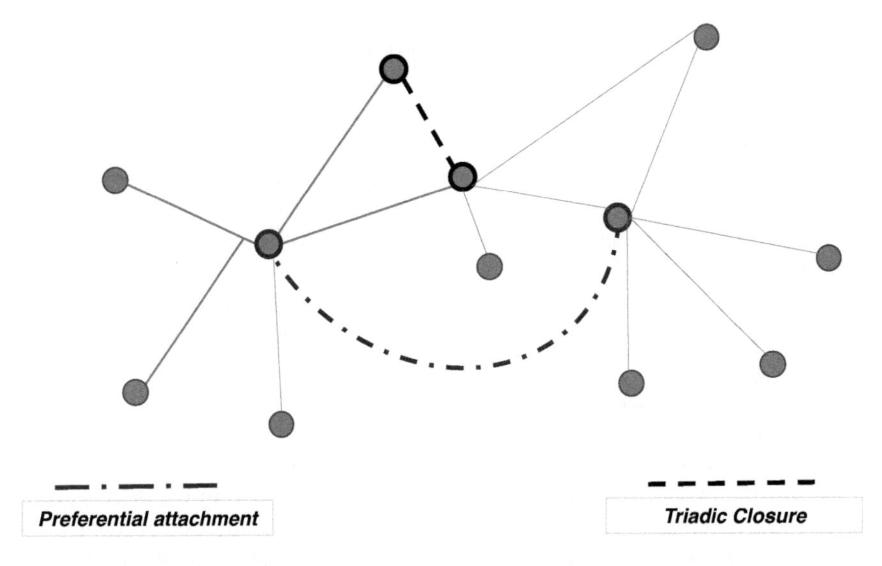

Figure 2.1 Networks' endogenous effects: preferential attachment; triadic closure
Source: Author's own elaboration from Glückler (2007)

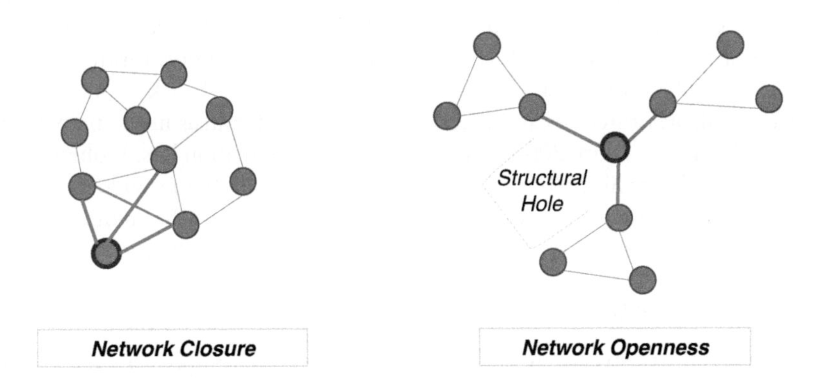

Figure 2.2 Coleman's network closure vs. Burt's structural hole
Source: Author's own elaboration

configurations of network structures are preferable in order to create social capital. Both visions agree on the definition of *social capital* as a type of capital that can generate a competitive advantage for specific individuals or groups in pursuing their ends. However, the debate contrasts the *closure argument*, according to which social capital is more likely to be created by a network where nodes are strongly connected to each other, and the *structural hole argument*, that supports the idea that social capital is generated through a network where nodes can broker connections between otherwise disconnected segments (Burt, 2002) (Figure 2.2).

2.3.1.1 *Network closure*

Coleman (1988, 1990) is one of the most prominent authors of the closure argument. His view emphasizes the importance of strong ties as they encourage the emergence of cooperative mechanisms and promote the development of shared social norms and trust and uncertainty reduction. Typically, closed and cohesive networks are characterized by frequent, reciprocal and repeated interactions where the involved parties usually have the possibility to cross-check information resulting from direct ties by the means of indirect paths in the network (Cassi, Morrison, & Ter Wal, 2012). The combination of these properties is deemed to generate trust mechanisms within partnerships of collaboration (Walker, Kogut, & Shan, 1997; Buskens, 2002; McEvily, Perrone, & Zaheer, 2003), which in turn strengthen the motivation and level of commitment to share knowledge within the relationship (Reagans & McEvily, 2003), with specific regard to the exchange of complex as well as sensitive knowledge (Zaheer & Bell, 2005). On this subject, Gargiulo and Benassi (2000) and Beckman, Haunschild and Phillips (2004) show how in situations of high levels of risk, market uncertainty and costs related to opportunistic behavior, actors tend to prefer to embed themselves in dense and close network structures, as in the case of US venture capital networks (Sorenson & Stuart, 2008). The repeated exchange among stable members is deemed to improve coordination and access to social capital. Therefore, the availability of social capital turns out to be function of the *closure* of the network surrounding them. In Coleman's view, closed networks are the source of social capital as they provide a better access to information and discourage opportunistic behavior (Coleman, 1988; Walker et al., 1997; Rowley, Behrens, & Krackhardt, 2000), as closure facilitates sanctions and reduces the risk of individuals in the network to trust each another (Burt, 2002) due to the threat of reputation loss. Cohesive and dense networks are likely to have similar information and thus provide redundant information benefits. Additionally, this perspective suggests that redundant ties among firms may result in a collective action's resolution of the problems.

2.3.1.2 *Structural holes*

Conversely, Burt's structural holes theory (2000, 2002) emphasizes the role of weak ties and the lack of network closure. The argument considers social capital as a function of brokerage opportunities and relies on concepts that originated in sociology during the 1970s, namely, the *strength of weak ties* (Granovetter, 1973) and *betweenness centrality* (Freeman, 1989). This perspective can be considered as an extension of Granovetter's argument about the strength of weak ties, which suggests that a greater amount of information is more easily obtained through weak rather than strong and long-term relationships. More specifically, the high costs related to the maintenance of close relationships would limit the number of "ties" that an organization can have. Second, since weak ties do not generally encompass a regular-basis interaction, they may access less redundant information compared to strong ties. Network *betweenness* is an index proposed by Freeman that indicates the extent to which a node brokers indirect connections among all

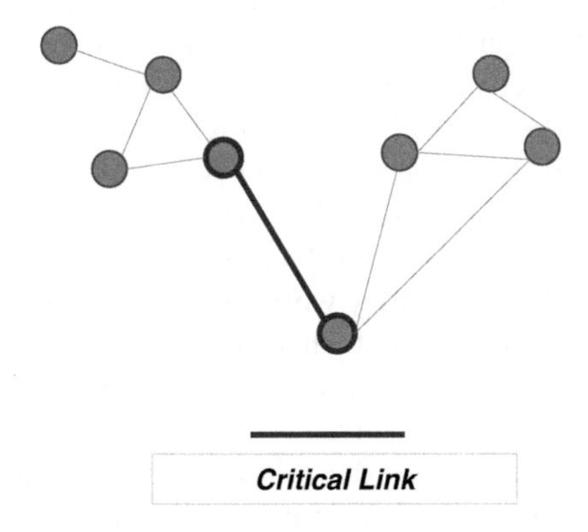

Figure 2.3 Critical links

Source: Author's own elaboration from Broekel & Mueller (2017)

other nodes in the network. The holes in social structure (i.e. structural holes) provide a competitive advantage for those actors whose connections span the holes, which in turn act as buffers separating non-redundant sources of information. Therefore, structural holes provide the possibility of brokering the flux of information between the nodes and "control the projects that bring together people from opposite sides of the hole" (Burt, 2002). Additionally, firms who are positioned in structural holes may have more opportunity to brokerage activities, by serving as bridges among relatively unconnected parts of the network. In the end, the availability of information is not limited to the function of a firm's ties only but also to those retained by third parties (i.e. network configuration). *Critical links* represent another class of ties that has gained increasing attention in the network literature (Figure 2.3). These links have the function of connecting poorly or otherwise disconnected sub-networks in a way that when they dissolve for some reason, the entire network collapses, including the process of knowledge transfer among its members. Due to the critical links' function to connect sparsely linked parts of the network, they have often been referred to as "bottlenecks" (Sytch, Tatarynowicz, & Gulati, 2012) or "bridges" (Glückler, 2007). However,

> while every critical link can be classified as a weak tie, the same is not necessarily true of the reverse. Critical links are crucial for the structure and integration of the complete network, while weak ties may only have local relevance.
>
> (Broekel & Mueller, 2017, p. 921)

2.3.1.3 *Gatekeeper organizations*

Tightly connected to the structural holes' argument and the importance of *critical links*, studies within systems of innovation literature have regarded with increasing interest the role of intermediary organizations (Hargadon & Sutton, 1997) or the so-called *gatekeeper* actors, which are defined as actors holding a brokerage position between an actor group's internal or external partners (Gould & Fernandez, 1989). With particular reference to their role within innovation networks, Allen (1977) introduces the definition of *technological gatekeeper*: an R&D professional provided with the particular intellectual ability to absorb information from external sources and make it available and accessible to other employees of the company that they work for. The brokerage position has been proved to positively impact the performance of those organizations that rely on them to access external information (Hargadon, 1998). More recently, the concept of gatekeeper has been transferred to the geographical context by Giuliani and Bell (2005), who emphasize the role of *regional gatekeepers* in embedding local systems of innovation in global innovation networks. More precisely, the innovation performance of regional systems of innovation is deemed to be highly affected by the presence of a small number of regional gatekeeper organizations (Giuliani & Bell, 2005; Graf & Krüger, 2011). Indeed, a growing number of scholars (see e.g. Gertler, 1997; Bathelt et al., 2004) recognize their important function in importing and diffusing new knowledge within the region, thus contributing to limit the risk of *lock-in phenomena* without preventing organizations from exploiting the benefits deriving from local *embeddedness* (Glückler, 2007). More specifically, Graf and Krüger (2011) emphasize the crucial role played by regional gatekeepers' absorptive capacity, which enables them to establish long-distance relationships to fill the cognitive gap existing between regional actors and external networks. Broekel and Mueller (2017) make a clear distinction between *network gatekeepers* and *regional gatekeepers*. While the former "are defined on the basis of a complete network" (p. 923), the latter are defined as organizations linking the regionally embedded network to an external network. Indeed, "while regional gatekeepers are always gatekeepers from a network perspective, the same does not necessarily apply the other way around" (Broekel & Mueller, 2017, p. 923). Morrison (2008) empirically verifies the tendency of regional gatekeepers to engage with organizations that are external to the region and specialized in complementary or similar assets and technologies, which suggests how cognitive proximity in this case may act as a substitute for geographic proximity and compensate for spatial distance.

2.3.1.4 Small worlds

Watts and Strogatz (1998) suggest that the structure of networks may present the benefits of both strong and weak ties. For this specific configuration, the authors refer to the *small worlds* (Travers & Milgram, 1967): particular types of networks characterized by a shorter path length and a higher clustering coefficient. In other words, in these networks the actors are close to almost all other elements through a smaller number of interconnecting paths, despite the large number of nodes (Figure 2.4). The first property of small worlds – *shorter path length* – sustains network closure, and for this reason it is expected that knowledge and

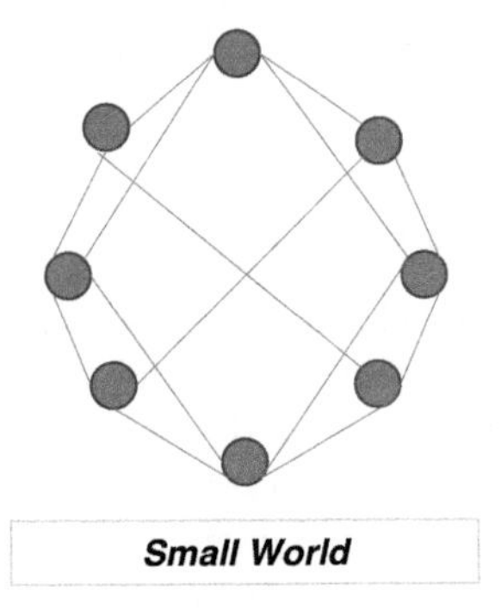

Figure 2.4 Small world network configuration
Source: Author's own elaboration

information circulate through the small world network more easily and quickly. Thus, a network with a small path length can be considered as one with fewer structural holes (benefit of weak ties). On the other hand, the second property – *higher clustering coefficient* – suggests that a larger social capital is accumulated, which leads to collective problem resolution (benefit of strong ties). However, following Ahuja (2000), the optimal structure of inter-firm networks ultimately depends on the objectives of the network members. The high degree of density and redundancy of linkages within local cliques ensures the formation of a common language and communication codes that enhance reciprocal trust and support the sharing of complex and tacit knowledge among actors (Breschi & Catalini, 2010); on the other hand, the shortcuts linking local cliques to different and weakly connected parts of the network ensures a rapid diffusion and recombination of new ideas throughout the network and allows keeping a window open to new sources of knowledge, thereby mitigating the risk of lock-in that could arise in the context of densely connected cliques (Cowan & Jonard, 2004).

2.4 The study of LIS through a network approach: a review

This section reviews a number of empirical studies adopting a network approach for the study of local innovation systems. The contributions are analyzed according to five main analytical dimensions: (1) the analytical perspective employed to trace the system's boundaries (sectorial, technological or geographical); (2) the network nodes' composition according to the nature of the actors engaged in the relationships; (3) the choices in terms of network portfolio of relationships that are used for the collection of relational data; (4) the scholars' position within the long-standing debate around the optimal network structure; (5) the choices about level of analysis (node/system); (6) the resulting network indicators (structural/centrality); and finally, when applicable, (7) the interpretation of innovation performance through the use of specific metrics. The next sections will discuss in details the aforementioned analytical aspects. A summary of the review is reported in Table 2.3.

2.4.1 *The definition of network boundaries*

Studies that analyze network characteristics generally focus on a single sector or on a particular geographic area, or a combination of the two. Some authors privilege to emphasize the sectorial dimension and focus their analysis on industry-related networks, as in the case of Salavisa et al. (2012), who argue that firms' networking behavior is generally affected by sectorial differences. Indeed, depending on the industry, firms are provided with different types, sources and modes of access to resources required for innovating, which in turn affects the whole network's architecture. More specifically, it is the *nature of knowledge* exploited and the *organization* of *innovative activities* to affect the type of resources required and the modes of access to them that ultimately influence the network architecture. From a more evolutionary perspective, Balland, Suire and Vicente (2013) focus their analysis on the emergence of inter-firm networks in the global video game industry and argue that the factors that drive network formation vary according to the stage of development in the industry life cycle. In particular, the authors find that organizations tend to partner over short distances (thus presenting a higher level of geographic proximity) and with organizations with more similar knowledge bases (i.e. in greater cognitive proximity) as the industry matures. Similarly, D'Este et al. (2012) investigate the role of geographic proximity in university-industry networks in the field of engineering and physical sciences in the UK. Finally, from a knowledge-based perspective, Capaldo and Petruzzelli (2014) explore the impact of geographic and organizational proximity on the innovative performance of 1,515 inter-firm dyadic knowledge-creating alliances in the electric and electronic equipment industry. Other contributions shift the focus on technology, as in the case of Balland (2012), which explores the global navigation satellite system (GNSS) to understand the influence of proximity on the evolution of collaboration networks in the framework of European Union R&D partnerships. Broekel and Mueller (2017) apply the proximity framework by empirically studying the characteristics of critical links in 132 technology-specific subsidized knowledge networks in Germany, demonstrating that critical links tend to emerge among inter-regional gatekeepers with similar knowledge bases and complementary resources. From an exclusively regional standpoint, Still, Huhtamäki, Russell and Rubens (2014) provide an analytical framework to understanding the network dynamics underlying the Finnish ecosystem at multiple levels for a heterogeneous sample of actors. Russell, Huhtamäki, Still, Rubens and Basole (2015) offer an evidence-based approach to exploring the relational infrastructure of spatially defined innovation systems in the three metropolitan areas of Austin (Texas, US), Minneapolis (Minnesota, US) and Paris (France). However, most of the reviewed empirical contributions tend to opt for the combination of both sector and regional perspectives, as in the case of Ahuja (2000), which develops a theoretical framework to relate the entrepreneurial innovation performance by taking evidence from the empirical study of collaborative linkages in Japan, the US and Western Europe in the chemical industry.

Owen-Smith and Powell (2004) explore the role of spatial propinquity and organizational form in altering the flow of information in the Boston biotechnology ecosystem by performing a network analysis on human therapeutics biotechnology firms located in the Boston metropolitan area, while Kajikawa, Takeda, Sakata and Matsushima (2010) conduct a comparative analysis on eight regional clusters in Japan to explore the role of bridging organizations in different industries. Similarly, Casanueva, Castro and Galán (2013) select the geographically localized footwear cluster in the region of Valverde (southern Spain) as an empirical context to study the effects of firms' position in the network on their innovation performance, while Ter Wal (2014) analyzes the evolution of inventor networks in German biotechnology, arguing that the role of geographical proximity decreases as the technological regime experiences a shift from tacit to more codified knowledge. An interesting contribution in this regard is that provided by Giuliani (2013), who employs the stochastic actor-oriented models (SAOM) to measure network dynamics and examine the micro-dynamics underlying the emergence of new knowledge ties in the Chilean wine cluster. Finally, Dahl and Pedersen (2004) explore the regional cluster of wireless communication firms in northern Denmark to study the effect of informal networks on innovation system dynamics of growth.

2.4.2 Network nodes' composition

It is well established in the literature of innovation systems that the heterogeneous nature of a system's components represents one of the main drivers of its performance. Previous sections have indeed focused on the advantages in terms of new knowledge production deriving from the exchanges of information, capabilities and experiences between actors of different nature and the virtuous cooperation practices through the industry–university–government (IUG) networks have been appointed as the engine for LIS emergence. From an empirical standpoint, the ability to capture (and assess) the diversity of actors' composition within innovation networks still remains a challenge. Except for a few cases (Dahl and Pedersen, 2004; Ter Wal, 2014) where the network analysis is conducted at the individual node level (i.e. inventors and engineers), a great part of the contributions that are reviewed in this chapter focus their analysis on inter-firm relationships, thus enabling to gain insights on the characteristics and dynamics of a certain aspect of the network and capture the specificities in more depth. Ahuja (2000) emphasizes the role of inter-firm networks as an information channel in terms of both *information collection* and *information processing*. More precisely, the network between firms is deemed to provide benefits as an information gathering device through which firms can obtain information about the successes and failures of contemporary research activities (Larsen &

Rogers, 1984), thus allowing to benefit from indirect experience and to avoid replicative efforts. Second, the network can act as an information processing or screening device through which, for example, a firm can detect relevant developments in complementary technologies to solving specific issues at hand. In light of this, Still et al. (2014) analyze the network of firms in Finland by focusing on the different roles and positions of larger and established companies, start-ups and investors, while Kajikawa et al. (2010) build a large dataset of firms to analyze the multiscale structures of eight inter-firm networks and compare their small world properties upon which classifying firms in hub or peripheral nodes. Russell et al. (2015) combines both the resource dependency and the coalition perspective, suggesting that inter-firm networks are complex systems characterized by "co-evolving actors engaged in collaboration and co-opetition . . . as well as the emergence of collective invention" (p. 7). Balland et al. (2013) study the dynamics of inter-firm networks along the game industry life cycle by including in their sample both *developers* and *publishers*, and Casanueva et al. (2013) explore the role of innovation networks in mature industries by studying relationships between 52 small and medium-sized firms presenting similar structural characteristics (size in terms of employee numbers), with specific regard to manufacturers and auxiliary firms. Additionally, Capaldo and Petruzzelli (2014) start from the identification of ten "focal" companies (based on their degree of innovativeness in the industry) to build the network resulting from focal companies' R&D alliances. Finally, Salavisa et al. (2012) focus on the network of R&D intensive small and medium-sized enterprises in software and biotech industries. However, network literature is showing an increasing commitment in analyzing LIS in their whole complexity by addressing the methodological challenges related to the study of diverse inter-organizational networks, starting from the study conducted by Owen-Smith and Powell (2004), who focus their attention on formal relationships between dedicated biotechnology firms, public research organizations, venture capital firms, government agencies and large companies in the pharmaceutical/chemical/healthcare industries. Balland (2012) includes, among the actors of the GNSS industry, organizations with heterogeneous institutional forms, including large companies, small and medium-sized enterprises, research institutes, public agencies or non-profit organizations. Similarly, D'Este et al. (2012) focus on research collaborations existing between university and industry. Finally, Broekel and Mueller (2017) investigate IUG networks for research grants by distinguishing among *executing* and *receiving* organizations, including (in the first category) large organizations as multinational companies and non-university research institutes.

2.4.3 Network portfolio of relationships

Extant literature acknowledges the existence of diverse types of relationships for the conduct of innovation-driven cooperation. However, partly due to methodology constraints, the study of formal ties appears to be prevalent with specific regard to R&D and commercial agreements, licensing agreements for technology transfer and patent co-development (Ahuja, 2000; Baum et al., 2000; Castilla, Hwang, Granovetter, & Granovetter, 2000; Cloodt, Hagedoorn, & Roijakkers, 2010; Gulati, 1995, 1999; Hanaki, Nakajima, & Ogura, 2010; Owen-Smith & Powell, 2004; Powell et al., 1996). With specific regard to the contributions that are reviewed in this session, a large number of the studies opt for R&D intensive relationships, as in the cases of Balland (2012) and Broekel and Mueller (2017) that rely on co-participation in R&D projects and subsidized joint R&D projects, respectively.

In this vein, D'Este et al. (2012) focus on publicly funded university-industry research partnerships as a preferential source of relational data, which are defined as "a transport vehicle of intended and unintended knowledge flows" (p. 543). In some cases (Ahuja, 2000), R&D partnerships are combined with financial relationships in the form of both direct and indirect ties to understand their effect on innovation performance. Capaldo and Petruzzelli (2014) and Ter Wal (2014) employ a particular type of knowledge-intensive alliances (i.e. joint patents), which are defined as an example of *knowledge-creating alliances* that differ from licensing and technology transfer that, in turn, are referred to as *knowledge-accessing* and *knowledge transfer alliances*, respectively. Indeed, according to the authors, "Being aimed at the joint development of new knowledge, knowledge-creating alliances require partners to combine heterogeneous knowledge and share knowledge resources that are complex and tacit to a large extent" (Capaldo and Petruzzelli 2014, p. 66), thus requiring a high level of interdependence. Similarly, Balland et al. (2013) rely on relationships for product co-development to collect relational data in the creative industry. Conversely, Kajikawa et al. (2010) focus on a more traditional set of customer-supply relationships. Other studies resort to a wider portfolio of relationships (Powell, 1996; Owen-Smith & Powell, 2004; Russell et al., 2015) spanning from R&D relationships and intellectual property (IP) transfer to commercial, manufacturing and investment ones. However, more recent contributions start to address the empirical challenges deriving from the analysis of informal networks (Arenius & De Clercq, 2005; Dahl & Pedersen, 2004; Kreiner & Schultz, 1993; McEvily & Zaheer, 1999; Østergaard, 2009; Shane & Cable, 2002; Weterings & Ponds, 2009), for which data are to a certain extent more difficult to collect. More precisely, the study of informal ties in reviewed contributions has been addressed by investigating interactions in the form of casual contacts between firms' employees (Dahl & Pedersen, 2004) or friendship, trust and tacit and explicit information exchange (Casanueva, 2013). Finally, some scholars adopt an aggregate approach (Cainelli, Mancinelli, & Mazzanti, 2007; Cantner, Meder, & Ter Wal, 2010; Elfring & Hulsink, 2003; Fuller-Love, 2009; Gilsing & Duysters, 2008; Giuliani & Bell, 2005; Yli-Renko, Autio, & Sapienza, 2001; Tödtling, Lehner, & Kaufmann, 2009; Zhao & Aram, 1995) by considering both types of formal and informal ties and eventually providing a comparative analysis (Cantner & Graf, 2006; Johannisson & Ramìrez-Pasillas, 2001; Tödtling et al., 2009; Trippl, Tödtling, & Lengauer, 2009; Uzzi, 1997, 1999). In a few cases the two typologies of networks are considered simultaneously, as in Salavisa et al. (2012), where the authors,

Table 2.2 Complementary assets and knowledge networks

	Formal	*Informal*
Complementary assets	Funding sources Facilities providers Service providers (legal, accounting, IP, marketing) Commercial partnerships	Managerial knowledge Information
Knowledge	R&D projects S&T partnerships Patents (partners, providers) Origin of the technology (if formally transferred)	Innovation (new ideas) S&T knowledge Origin of technology (if informally transferred)

Source: Author's own elaboration from Salavisa et al. (2012)

while comparing the sectorial differences in two German knowledge networks in the fields of molecular biology and software for telecommunications, studied both formal and informal networks and distinguished them according to the type of resources that they allow to capture (i.e. *complementary assets* and *knowledge*; Table 2.2). The complementary asset network includes all relationships to acquire both tangible resources (e.g. financial capital, distribution channels, equipment and facilities) and intangible ones (e.g. business management knowledge, information, consultancy services), and include *commercial partnerships, service provision* (legal, accounting, IP, marketing), *agreements for the provision of facilities* and *funding relations*. On the other hand, the knowledge network consists of all relationships that allow knowledge and technology transfer and production as in the case of R&D projects, S&T partnerships, patents (partners and providers) and licensing agreements.

In addition to the resource type, the authors distinguish the nature of the relations as informal or formal. While the latter refer to codified agreements with a clear definition of roles and duties through contracts, informal relationships generally originate from personal ties and spontaneously. However, the scholars argue that the difference is not always clear-cut and that, in some cases, the actors may establish both forms of ties with the same organization, especially when "formal ties are frequently based on previous informal relations" (Salavisa et al., 2012, p. 388).

2.4.4 *Network structure perspective*

While adopting a network approach for the study of industry-related networks, a significant part of existing literature focus their analysis at the firm level (Casanueva et al., 2013), suggesting that the position in the network, expressed in metrics of centrality, influences its innovative performance as it allows for a greater access to information (Gulati, 1999; Owen-Smith & Powell, 2004), generates positive effects on organizational learning and reputation (Powell et al., 1996) and increases the number of its direct ties (Ahuja, 2000). More recent contributions emphasize the geographical dimension and provide a wider range of indicators not limited to the organization's position within the network, but also structural metrics at the network level to assess the performance of the cluster as a whole (Balland et al., 2013; Balland, 2012; Capaldo & Petruzzelli, 2014; D'Este et al., 2012; Dahl & Pedersen, 2004; Powell et al., 1996; Still et al., 2013; Ter Wal, 2014; Cassi & Plunket, 2014). In other cases, a combination of both structural and positional metrics have been used to capture insights at both node and system levels (Ahuja, 2000; Broekel & Mueller, 2017; Giuliani, 2013; Kajikawa et al., 2010; Owen-Smith & Powell, 2004; Russell et al., 2015; Salavisa et al., 2012). As for the structural perspective, the majority of the studies under review opt for a closed approach (Balland et al., 2013; Balland, 2012; Capaldo & Petruzzelli, 2014; Cassi & Plunket, 2014; D'Este et al., 2012; Owen-Smith & Powell, 2004; Powell et al., 1996; Russell et al., 2015; Still et al., 2013), while the open argument has been chosen as a standpoint in a fewer number of studies (Broekel & Mueller, 2017; Casanueva et al., 2013; Dahl & Pedersen, 2004; Ter Wal, 2014). In one case, the small world perspective is implemented (Kajikawa, 2010). Finally, Salavisa et al. (2012) and Giuliani (2013) present a mixed approach, combining the strengths and the pitfalls of both views.

2.4.5 The relationship between network characteristics and innovation performance

Extant literature provides a number of contributions that address the relationship between network characteristics and innovation performance. Empirical findings, in general, support the theoretical relation (Bell, 2005; Bell & Zaheer, 2007; Chiu, 2008) between centrality and innovation, which has been widely explored and validated in the literature (Ahuja, 2000; Tsai, 2001). Innovation outcomes have been interpreted in a number of ways, such as alliance governance (Dyer & Singh, 1998; Sampson, 2004), characteristics of the search processes conducted within the alliances (Capaldo & Petruzzelli, 2011) and various aspects of the inter-organizational networks where the relationships are embedded (Ahuja, 2000; Baum et al., 2000; Capaldo, 2007). However, the performance of inter-organizational networks still remains a relatively unexplored area (Osborn & Hagedoorn, 1997) with specific regard to innovative performance of alliances (Hoang & Rothaermel, 2005). Powell et al. (1996) measure innovation performance in terms of ability to establish future R&D alliances and to contribute to a firm's growth. Ahuja (2000) assesses the effects of a firm's ego network on innovation by developing a theoretical framework that associates three specific characteristics of a firm's ego network: direct ties, indirect ties and structural holes to the firm's innovation output, which is measured in terms of patents. In a similar vein, Owen-Smith and Powell (2004) demonstrate how membership and centrality in a geographically co-located

Table 2.3 Empirical studies adopting a network approach for the study of local innovation systems

	Analytical perspective	*SNA metrics*	*SNA approach*	*Type of ties*	*Network portfolio*	*Nodes*	*Innovation performance metrics*
Ahuja (2000)	Sectorial/ regional	Structural/ positional	Closure/ open	Formal	Finance, R&D	Firms	Patents
Balland et al. (2013)	Sectorial	Structural	Closure	Formal	Product co-development	Firms	–
Balland (2012)	Sectorial	Structural	Closure	Formal	Co-participation in EU R&D projects	Large companies, small and medium-sized enterprises, research institutes, public agencies or non-profit organizations	–
Broekel and Mueller (2017)	Sectorial/ technological	Structural/ positional	Open	Informal	Subsidized joint R&D projects	Universities, firms, research institutes and miscellaneous organizations	–
Capaldo and Messeni Petruzzelli (2014)	Sectorial	Structural	Closure	Formal	Joint patents	Firms	Number of patent citations
Casanueva et al. (2013)	Sectorial/ regional	Structural	Open	Informal	Transmission of tacit and explicit knowledge	Firms	Product and process innovation
Cassi and Plunket (2014)	Regional	Structural	Closure	Formal	Co-inventorship relations	Individuals	–
D'Este et al. (2012)	Sectorial	Structural	Closure	Formal	Collaborative research grants	Universities and firms	–
Dahl and Pedersen (2004)	Sectorial/ regional	Structural	Open	Informal	Information exchange	Individuals (engineers)	–

Giuliani (2013)	Sectorial/ regional	Structural/ positional	Mixed approach	Informal	Technical support (inbound and outbound)	Firms	–
Kajikawa et al. (2010)	Sectorial/ regional	Structural/ positional	Small worlds	Formal	Customer-supply relationships	Firms	–
Owen-Smith and Powell (2004)	Sectorial/ regional	Structural/ positional	Closure	Formal	R&D, finance, commercial and IP transfer	Firms, government agencies, public research organizations and venture capital	
Powell, Koput, and Smith-Doerr (1996)	Sectorial	Positional	Closure	Formal	R&D, finance, commercial, custom-supply and IP transfer	Firms	# R&D ties ($t + 1$); growth ($t + 1$)
Russell et al. (2015)	Regional	Structural/ positional	Closure	Formal	R&D, finance, commercial, custom-supply, IP transfer and manufacturing	Firms	–
Salavisa et al. (2012)	Sectorial	Structural/ positional	Mixed approach	Formal	Knowledge and complementary asset relationships	Firms	–
Still et al. (2013)	Regional	Structural	Closure	Formal	R&D, finance, commercial, custom-supply, IP transfer and manufacturing	Firms	–
Ter Wal (2014)	Sectorial/ regional	Structural	Open	Formal	Co-inventorship relations	Individuals	–

Source: Author's own elaboration

network positively affects innovation by appointing patents as a proxy for innovation performance.

Capaldo and Petruzzelli (2014) explore the effects of geographic propinquity on knowledge-intensive alliances' performance by considering the number of citations of joint patents (used as relational data) as an appropriate metric for innovation performance. Finally, Casanueva et al. (2013) analyze the influence of centrality and structural holes in tacit and explicit knowledge networks on firms' innovation performance, this being measured in terms of product and process innovation.

2.5 Literature gap and summary

This chapter aims to explore the key concepts underpinning the relational dimension as a driver of LIS performance and to illustrate the relative analytical challenges through the analysis of main contributions in the field. Based on reviewed studies in previous sections, the following gaps in the literature have been identified:

- There is no general agreement on the optimal configuration of network structure (e.g. closure network vs. structural holes);
- Most contributions employing a network approach for the study of innovation systems' performance limit their analysis at the node level and mainly focus on inter-firm relationships, thus overlooking the heterogeneous nature of a system's components, which is an important driver for the production of new knowledge;
- Most studies limit their analysis to strong and formal ties, overlooking the potential for informal and weaker ties;
- Extant literature tends to limit the analysis to network structure and does not address the variety of inter-organizational relationships, thus failing to gain insights into the optimal network portfolio composition.

In order to fill these gaps and in an attempt to capture both aspects of LIS's relational dimension (network structure and network portfolio composition), the following chapters will explore:

(RQ1) What is the configuration of the network structure of a successful local innovation system?
(RQ2) What is the portfolio of relationships implemented in a successful local innovation system?

Chapter 3 will provide a more in-depth explanation of the reasons underpinning the formulation of these research questions and address the relative methodological challenges through the development of an exploratory study of the biopharma innovation system in the Greater Boston Area.

References

Abramovsky, L., & Simpson, H. (2011). Geographic proximity and firm–university innovation linkages: Evidence from Great Britain. *Journal of Economic Geography, 11*(6), 949–977.

Agrawal, A., Cockburn, I., & McHale, J. (2006). Gone but not forgotten: Knowledge flows, labor mobility, and enduring social relationships. *Journal of Economic Geography, 6*(5), 571–591.

Ahuja, G. (2000). Collaboration networks, structural holes, and innovation: A longitudinal study. *Administrative Science Quarterly, 45*(3), 425–455.

Aldrich, H., Zimmer, C., & Jones, T. (1986). Small business still speaks with the same voice: A replication of "the voice of small business and the politics of survival". *The Sociological Review, 34*(2), 335–356.

Allen, T. J. (1977). Managing the flow of technology: Technology transfer and the dissemination of technological information within the R and D organization. *MIT Press Books, 1.*

Arenius, P., & De Clercq, D. (2005). A network-based approach on opportunity recognition. *Small Business Economics, 24*(3), 249–265.

Arora, R. (2002). Implementing KM: A balanced score card approach. *Journal of Knowledge Management, 6*(3), 240–249.

Audretsch, D. B., & Feldman, M. P. (1996). R&D spillovers and the geography of innovation and production. *The American Economic Review, 86*(3), 630–640.

Balland, P. A. (2012). Proximity and the evolution of collaboration networks: Evidence from research and development projects within the global navigation satellite system (GNSS) industry. *Regional Studies, 46*(6), 741–756.

Balland, P. A., De Vaan, M., & Boschma, R. (2012). The dynamics of interfirm networks along the industry life cycle: The case of the global video game industry, 1987–2007. *Journal of Economic Geography, 13*(5), 741–765.

Balland, P. A., Suire, R., & Vicente, J. (2013). Structural and geographical patterns of knowledge networks in emerging technological standards: Evidence from the European GNSS industry. *Economics of Innovation and New Technology, 22*(1), 47–72.

Barabási, A. L., & Albert, R. (1999). Emergence of scaling in random networks. *Science, 286*(5439), 509–512.

Bathelt, H., & Glückler, J. (2003). Toward a relational economic geography. *Journal of Economic Geography, 3*(2), 117–144.

Bathelt, H., Malmberg, A., & Maskell, P. (2004). Clusters and knowledge: Local buzz, global pipelines and the process of knowledge creation. *Progress in Human Geography, 28*(1), 31–56.

Baum, J. A., Calabrese, T., & Silverman, B. S. (2000). Don't go it alone: Alliance network composition and startups' performance in Canadian biotechnology. *Strategic Management Journal, 21*(3), 267–294.

Becattini, G., Bellandi, M., & De Propris, L. (Eds.). (2014). *A handbook of industrial districts.* Cheltenham: Edward Elgar.

Beckman, C. M., Haunschild, P. R., & Phillips, D. J. (2004). Friends or strangers? Firm-specific uncertainty, market uncertainty, and network partner selection. *Organization Science, 15*(3), 259–275.

Bell, G. G. (2005). Clusters, networks, and firm innovativeness. *Strategic Management Journal, 26*(3), 287–295.

Bell, G. G., & Zaheer, A. (2007). Geography, networks, and knowledge flow. *Organization Science, 18*(6), 955–972.

Ben Lataifa, S., & Rabeau, Y. (2013). Too close to collaborate? How geographical proximity could impede entrepreneurship and innovation. *Journal of Business Research, 33.* http://dx.doi.org/10.1016/j.jburses.

Bergman, E. M. (2009). Embedding network analysis in spatial studies of innovation. *The Annals of Regional Science, 43*(3), 559–565.

Boschma, R. (2005). Proximity and innovation: A critical assessment. *Regional Studies, 39*(1), 61–74.

Breschi, S., & Catalini, C. (2010). Tracing the links between science and technology: An exploratory analysis of scientists' and inventors' networks. *Research Policy, 39*(1), 14–26.

Breschi, S., Lenzi, C., Lissoni, F., & Vezzulli, A. (2010). The geography of knowledge spillovers: The role of inventors' mobility across firms and in space. In *The handbook of evolutionary economic geography* (pp. 353–369). Cheltenham: Edward Elgar.

Broekel, T., & Boschma, R. (2011). Knowledge networks in the Dutch aviation industry: The proximity paradox. *Journal of Economic Geography, 12*(2), 409–433.

Broekel, T., & Mueller, W. (2018). Critical links in knowledge networks: What about proximities and gatekeeper organizations? *Industry and Innovation, 25*(10), 919–939.

Burt, R. S. (2000). The network structure of social capital. *Research in Organizational Behavior, 22*, 345–423.

Burt, R. S. (2002). Bridge decay. *Social Networks, 24*(4), 333–363.

Buskens, V. (2002). *Social networks and trust* (Vol. 30). Springer Science & Business Media.

Cainelli, G., Mancinelli, S., & Mazzanti, M. (2007). Social capital and innovation dynamics in district-based local systems. *The Journal of Socio-Economics, 36*(6), 932–948.

Cantner, U., & Graf, H. (2006). The network of innovators in Jena: An application of social network analysis. *Research Policy, 35*(4), 463–480.

Cantner, U., Meder, A., & Ter Wal, A. L. (2010). Innovator networks and regional knowledge base. *Technovation, 30*(9), 496–507.

Capaldo, A. (2007). Network structure and innovation: The leveraging of a dual network as a distinctive relational capability. *Strategic Management Journal, 28*(6), 585–608.

Capaldo, A., & Petruzzelli, A. M. (2011). In search of alliance-level relational capabilities: Balancing innovation value creation and appropriability in R&D alliances. *Scandinavian Journal of Management, 27*(3), 273–286.

Capaldo, A., & Petruzzelli, A. M. (2014). Partner geographic and organizational proximity and the innovative performance of knowledge-creating alliances. *European Management Review, 11*(1), 63–84.

Carrincazeaux, C., Grossetti, M., & Talbot, D. (2008). Clusters, proximities and networks. *European Planning Studies, 16*(5), 613–616.

Casanueva, C., Castro, I., & Galán, J. L. (2013). Informational networks and innovation in mature industrial clusters. *Journal of Business Research, 66*(5), 603–613.

Cassi, L., Morrison, A., & Ter Wal, A. L. (2012). The evolution of trade and scientific collaboration networks in the global wine sector: A longitudinal study using network analysis. *Economic Geography, 88*(3), 311–334.

Cassi, L., & Plunket, A. (2014). Proximity, network formation and inventive performance: In search of the proximity paradox. *The Annals of Regional Science, 53*(2), 395–422.

Castilla, E. J., Hwang, H., Granovetter, E., & Granovetter, M. (2000). Social networks in Silicon Valley. *The Silicon Valley Edge*, 218–247.

Chiu, Y. (2008). How network competence and network location influence innovation performance. *Journal of Business and Industrial Marketing, 24*(1), 46–55.

Cloodt, M., Hagedoorn, J., & Roijakkers, N. (2010). Inter-firm R&D networks in the global software industry: An overview of major trends and patterns. *Business History, 52*(1), 120–149.

Cohen, W. M., & Levinthal, D. A. (1990). Absorptive capacity: A new perspective on learning and innovation. *Administrative Science Quarterly*, 128–152.

Coleman, J. S. (1988). Social capital in the creation of human capital. *American Journal of Sociology, 94*, S95–S120.

Coleman, J. S. (1990). *Foundations of social theory*. Cambridge, MA: Belknap Press of Harvard University Press.

Cowan, R., & Jonard, N. (2004). Network structure and the diffusion of knowledge. *Journal of Economic Dynamics and Control, 28*(8), 1557–1575.

Dahl, M. S., & Pedersen, C. Ø. (2004). Knowledge flows through informal contacts in industrial clusters: Myth or reality? *Research Policy, 33*(10), 1673–1686.

Davis, D., Davis, M. E., Jadad, A., Perrier, L., Rath, D., Ryan, D., . . . Zwarenstein, M. (2003). The case for knowledge translation: Shortening the journey from evidence to effect. *BMJ, 327*(7405), 33–35.

Davis, S. (1970). Building talented teams. *Innovation, 15*, 1–20.

DeBresson, C., & Amesse, F. (1991). Networks of innovators: A review and introduction to the issue. *Research Policy, 20*(5), 363–379.

D'Este, P., Guy, F., & Iammarino, S. (2012). Shaping the formation of university–industry research collaborations: What type of proximity does really matter? *Journal of Economic Geography, 13*(4), 537–558.

Dicken, P., Kelly, P. F., Olds, K., & Wai-Chung Yeung, H. (2001). Chains and networks, territories and scales: Towards a relational framework for analysing the global economy. *Global Networks, 1*(2), 89–112.

Dyer, J. H., & Singh, H. (1998). The relational view: Cooperative strategy and sources of interorganizational competitive advantage. *Academy of Management Review, 23*(4), 660–679.

Edquist, C., & Johnson, B. (1997). System of innovation: Overview and basic concepts. In *Systems of innovation: Technologies, institutions and organizations*. London: Routledge.

Eisenhardt, K. M., & Schoonhoven, C. B. (1996). Resource-based view of strategic alliance formation: Strategic and social effects in entrepreneurial firms. *Organization Science, 7*(2), 136–150.

Elfring, T., & Hulsink, W. (2003). Networks in entrepreneurship: The case of high-technology firms. *Small Business Economics, 21*(4), 409–422.

Fagerberg, J., Martin, B. R., & Andersen, E. S. (Eds.). (2013). *Innovation studies: Evolution and future challenges*. Oxford: Oxford University Press.

Fitjar, R. D., Huber, F., & Rodríguez-Pose, A. (2016). Not too close, not too far: Testing the Goldilocks principle of "optimal" distance in innovation networks. *Industry and Innovation, 23*(6), 465–487.

Freeman, C. (1989). *Technology policy and economic performance*. London: Pinter.

Freeman, C. (2002). Continental, national and sub-national innovation systems: Complementarity and economic growth. *Research Policy, 31*(2), 191–211.

Fuller-Love, N. (2009). Formal and informal networks in small businesses in the media industry. *International Entrepreneurship and Management Journal, 5*(3), 271–284.

Gargiulo, M., & Benassi, M. (2000). Trapped in your own net? Network cohesion, structural holes, and the adaptation of social capital. *Organization Science, 11*(2), 183–196.

Geldes, C., Felzensztein, C., Turkina, E., & Durand, A. (2015). How does proximity affect interfirm marketing cooperation? A study of an agribusiness cluster. *Journal of Business Research, 68*(2), 263–272.

Gertler, M. (1997). The invention of regional culture. *Geographies of Economies*, 47–58.

Gilly, J. P., & Torre, A. (2000). Proximity relations. Elements for an analytical framework. *Industrial Networks and Proximity*, 1–16.

Gilsing, V. A., & Duysters, G. M. (2008). Understanding novelty creation in exploration networks: Structural and relational embeddedness jointly considered. *Technovation, 28*(10), 693–708.

Giuliani, E. (2013). Network dynamics in regional clusters: Evidence from Chile. Research *Policy, 42*(8), 1406–1419.

Giuliani, E., & Bell, M. (2005). The micro-determinants of meso-level learning and innovation: Evidence from a Chilean wine cluster. *Research Policy, 34*(1), 47–68.

Glückler, J. (2007). Economic geography and the evolution of networks. *Journal of Economic Geography*, 7(5), 619–634.

Gould, R. V., & Fernandez, R. M. (1989). Structures of mediation: A formal approach to brokerage in transaction networks. *Sociological Methodology*, 89–126.

Grabher, G. (2006). Trading routes, bypasses, and risky intersections: Mapping the travels of "networks" between economic sociology and economic geography. *Progress in Human Geography, 30*(2), 163–189.

Grabher, G., & Ibert, O. (2006). 2006: Bad company? The ambiguity of personal knowledge networks. *Journal of Economic Geography, 6*, 251–271.

Graf, H., & Krüger, J. J. (2011). The performance of gatekeepers in innovator networks. *Industry and Innovation, 18*(1), 69–88.

Granovetter, M. S. (1973). The strength of weak ties. *American Journal of Sociology, 78*(6), 1360–1380.

Granovetter, M. S. (1985). Economic action and social structure: The problem of embeddedness. *American Journal of Sociology, 91*(3), 481–510.

Gulati, R. (1995). Social structure and alliance formation patterns: A longitudinal analysis. *Administrative Science Quarterly*, 619–652.

Gulati, R. (1999). Network location and learning: The influence of network resources and firm capabilities on alliance formation. *Strategic Management Journal, 20*(5), 397–420.

Gulati, R., & Gargiulo, M. (1999). Where do interorganizational networks come from? *American Journal of Sociology, 104*(5), 1439–1493.

Halinen, A. (2012). *Relationship marketing in professional services: A study of agency-client dynamics in the advertising sector.* London: Routledge.

Hanaki, N., Nakajima, R., & Ogura, Y. (2010). The dynamics of R&D network in the IT industry. *Research Policy, 39*(3), 386–399.

Hargadon, A. B. (1998). Firms as knowledge brokers: Lessons in pursuing continuous innovation. *California Management Review, 40*(3), 209–227.

Hargadon, A. B., & Sutton, R. I. (1997). Technology brokering and innovation in a product development firm. *Administrative Science Quarterly*, 716–749.

Hoang, H., & Rothaermel, F. T. (2005). The effect of general and partner-specific alliance experience on joint R&D project performance. *Academy of Management Journal, 48*(2), 332–345.

Holland, P. W., & Leinhardt, S. (1971). Transitivity in structural models of small groups. *Comparative Group Studies, 2*(2), 107–124.

Howells, J. R. (2002). Tacit knowledge, innovation and economic geography. *Urban Studies, 39*(5–6), 871–884.

Huang, H. C., Lai, M. C., & Lo, K. W. (2012). Do founders' own resources matter? The influence of business networks on start-up innovation and performance. *Technovation, 32*(5), 316–327.

Huber, F. (2012). On the role and interrelationship of spatial, social and cognitive proximity: Personal knowledge relationships of R&D workers in the Cambridge information technology cluster. *Regional Studies, 46*(9), 1169–1182.

Johannisson, B., & Ramìrez-Pasillas, M. (2001). Networking for entrepreneurship: Building a topography model of human, social and cultural capital. *Frontiers of Entrepreneurship Research*. 21st, Annual entrepreneurship research conference; 2001; Jonkoping, Sweden.

Kajikawa, Y., Takeda, Y., Sakata, I., & Matsushima, K. (2010). Multiscale analysis of interfirm networks in regional clusters. *Technovation*, *30*(3), 168–180.

Kirat, T., & Lung, Y. (1999). Innovation and proximity: Territories as loci of collective learning processes. *European Urban and Regional Studies*, *6*(1), 27–38.

Knoben, J., & Oerlemans, L. A. (2006). Proximity and inter-organizational collaboration: A literature review. *International Journal of Management Reviews*, *8*(2), 71–89.

Kreiner, K., & Schultz, M. (1993). Informal collaboration in R&D. The formation of networks across organizations. *Organization Studies*, *14*(2), 189–209.

Larsen, J. K., & Rogers, E. M. (1984). *Silicon Valley fever: Growth of high-technology culture*. New York: Basic Books.

Maggioni, M. A., Nosvelli, M., & Uberti, T. E. (2007). Space versus networks in the geography of innovation: A European analysis. *Papers in Regional Science*, *86*(3), 471–493.

McEvily, B., Perrone, V., & Zaheer, A. (2003). Trust as an organizing principle. *Organization Science*, *14*(1), 91–103.

McEvily, B., & Zaheer, A. (1999). Bridging ties: A source of firm heterogeneity in competitive capabilities. *Strategic Management Journal*, 1133–1156.

McPherson, M., Smith-Lovin, L., & Cook, J. M. (2001). Birds of a feather: Homophily in social networks. *Annual Review of Sociology*, *27*(1), 415–444.

Mizruchi, M. S. (1992). *The structure of corporate political action: Interfirm relations and their consequences*. Cambridge, MA: Harvard University Press.

Moensted, M. (2007). Strategic networking in small high tech firms. *International Entrepreneurship and Management Journal*, *3*(1), 15–27.

Molina-Morales, F. X., Belso-Martínez, J. A., Más-Verdú, F., & Martínez-Cháfer, L. (2015). Formation and dissolution of inter-firm linkages in lengthy and stable networks in clusters. *Journal of Business Research*, *68*(7), 1557–1562.

Molina-Morales, F. X., García-Villaverde, P. M., & Parra-Requena, G. (2014). Geographical and cognitive proximity effects on innovation performance in SMEs: A way through knowledge acquisition. *International Entrepreneurship and Management Journal*, *10*(2), 231–251.

Moody, J., & White, D. R. (2003). Structural cohesion and embeddedness: A hierarchical concept of social groups. *American Sociological Review*, 103–127.

Morgan, K. (2004). The exaggerated death of geography: Learning, proximity and territorial innovation systems. *Journal of Economic Geography*, *4*(1), 3–21.

Morrison, A. (2008). Gatekeepers of knowledge within industrial districts: Who they are, how they interact. *Regional Studies*, *42*(6), 817–835.

Murdoch, J. (2000). Networks: A new paradigm of rural development? *Journal of Rural Studies*, *16*(4), 407–419.

Nooteboom, B. (1999). Innovation and inter-firm linkages: New implications for policy. *Research Policy*, *28*(8), 793–805.

Nooteboom, B. (2000). Learning by interaction: Absorptive capacity, cognitive distance and governance. *Journal of Management and Governance*, *4*(1–2), 69–92.

Oerlemans, L., & Meeus, M. (2005). Do organizational and spatial proximity impact on firm performance? *Regional Studies*, *39*(1), 89–104.

Osborn, R. N., & Hagedoorn, J. (1997). The institutionalization and evolutionary dynamics of interorganizational alliances and networks. *Academy of Management Journal*, *40*(2), 261–278.

Østergaard, C. R. (2009). Knowledge flows through social networks in a cluster: Comparing university and industry links. *Structural Change and Economic Dynamics*, *20*(3), 196–210.

Owen-Smith, J., & Powell, W. W. (2004). Knowledge networks as channels and conduits: The effects of spillovers in the Boston biotechnology community. *Organization Science, 15*(1), 5–21.

Ozman, M. (2009). Inter-firm networks and innovation: A survey of literature. *Economic of Innovation and New Technology, 18*(1), 39–67.

Polanyi, K. (1944). *The great transformation: Economic and political origins of our time.* New York: Rinehart.

Ponds, R., Van Oort, F., & Frenken, K. (2007). The geographical and institutional proximity of research collaboration. *Papers in Regional Science, 86*(3), 423–443.

Porter, M. E. (1998). *Clusters and the new economics of competition* (Vol. 76, No. 6, pp. 77–90). Boston, MA: Harvard Business Review.

Powell, W. W., Koput, K. W., & Smith-Doerr, L. (1996). Interorganizational collaboration and the locus of innovation: Networks of learning in biotechnology. *Administrative Science Quarterly*, 116–145.

Powell, W. W., Koput, K. W., Smith-Doerr, L., & Owen-Smith, J. (1999). Network position and firm performance: Organizational returns to collaboration in the biotechnology industry. *Research in the Sociology of Organizations, 16*(1), 129–159.

Presutti, M., Boari, C., & Majocchi, A. (2013). Inter-organizational geographical proximity and local start-ups' knowledge acquisition: A contingency approach. *Entrepreneurship and Regional Development, 25*(5–6), 446–467.

Reagans, R., & McEvily, B. (2003). Network structure and knowledge transfer: The effects of cohesion and range. *Administrative Science Quarterly, 48*(2), 240–267.

Ritter, T., & Gemünden, H. G. (2003). Network competence: Its impact on innovation success and its antecedents. *Journal of Business Research, 56*(9), 745–755.

Rosenthal, S. S., & Strange, W. C. (2001). The determinants of agglomeration. *Journal of Urban Economics, 50*(2), 191–229.

Rowley, T., Behrens, D., & Krackhardt, D. (2000). Redundant governance structures: An analysis of structural and relational embeddedness in the steel and semiconductor industries. *Strategic Management Journal, 21*(3), 369–386.

Russell, M. G., Huhtamäki, J., Still, K., Rubens, N., & Basole, R. C. (2015). Relational capital for shared vision in innovation ecosystems. *Triple Helix, 2*(1), 1–36.

Russell, M. G., Still, K., Huhtamäki, J., Yu, C., & Rubens, N. (2011). Transforming innovation ecosystems through shared vision and network orchestration. In *Triple Helix IX International Conference*, Stanford, CA, USA.

Salavisa, I., Sousa, C., & Fontes, M. (2012). Topologies of innovation networks in knowledge-intensive sectors: Sectoral differences in the access to knowledge and complementary assets through formal and informal ties. *Technovation, 32*(6), 380–399.

Sampson, R. C. (2004). Organizational choice in R&D alliances: Knowledge-based and transaction cost perspectives. *Managerial and Decision Economics, 25*(6–7), 421–436.

Shane, S., & Cable, D. (2002). Network ties, reputation, and the financing of new ventures. *Management Science, 48*(3), 364–381.

Singh, J. (2005). Collaborative networks as determinants of knowledge diffusion patterns. *Management Science, 51*(5), 756–770.

Sorenson, O., Rivkin, J. W., & Fleming, L. (2006). Complexity, networks and knowledge flow. *Research Policy, 35*(7), 994–1017.

Sorenson, O., & Stuart, T. E. (2008). Bringing the context back in: Settings and the search for syndicate partners in venture capital investment networks. *Administrative Science Quarterly, 53*(2), 266–294.

Still, K., Huhtamäki, J., Russell, M. G., & Rubens, N. (2014). Insights for orchestrating innovation ecosystems: The case of EIT ICT Labs and data-driven network visualisations. *International Journal of Technology Management*, *66*(2–3), 243–265.

Stuart, T., & Sorenson, O. (2003). The geography of opportunity: Spatial heterogeneity in founding rates and the performance of biotechnology firms. *Research Policy*, *32*(2), 229–253.

Sunley, P. (2008). Relational economic geography: A partial understanding or a new paradigm? *Economic Geography*, *84*(1), 1–26.

Sytch, M., Tatarynowicz, A., & Gulati, R. (2012). Toward a theory of extended contact: The incentives and opportunities for bridging across network communities. *Organization Science*, *23*(6), 1658–1681.

Tallman, S., Jenkins, M., Henry, N., & Pinch, S. (2004). Knowledge, clusters, and competitive advantage. *Academy of Management Review*, *29*(2), 258–271.

Teece, D. J. (1986). Profiting from technological innovation: Implications for integration, collaboration, licensing and public policy. *Research Policy*, *15*(6), 285–305.

Ter Wal, A. L. J. (2014). The dynamics of the inventor network in German biotechnology: Geographic proximity versus triadic closure. *Journal of Economic Geography*, *14*(3), 589–620.

Ter Wal, A. L. J., & Boschma, R. A. (2009). Applying social network analysis in economic geography: Framing some key analytic issues. *The Annals of Regional Science*, *43*(3), 739–756.

Tödtling, F., Lehner, P., & Kaufmann, A. (2009). Do different types of innovation rely on specific kinds of knowledge interactions? *Technovation*, *29*(1), 59–71.

Torre, A. (2008). On the role played by temporary geographical proximity in knowledge transmission. *Regional Studies*, *42*(6), 869–889.

Torre, A., & Rallet, A. (2005). Proximity and localization. *Regional Studies*, *39*(1), 47–59.

Travers, J., & Milgram, S. (1967). The small world problem. *Psychology Today*, *1*, 61–67.

Trippl, M., Tödtling, F., & Lengauer, L. (2009). Knowledge sourcing beyond buzz and pipelines: Evidence from the Vienna software sector. *Economic Geography*, *85*(4), 443–462.

Tsai, W. (2001). Knowledge transfer in intraorganizational networks: Effects of network position and absorptive capacity on business unit innovation and performance. *Academy of Management Journal*, *44*(5), 996–1004.

Uzzi, B. (1996). The sources and consequences of embeddedness for the economic performance of organizations: The network effect. *American Sociological Review*, 674–698.

Uzzi, B. (1997). Social structure and competition in interfirm networks: The paradox of embeddedness. *Administrative Science Quarterly*, 35–67.

Uzzi, B. (1999). Embeddedness in the making of financial capital: How social relations and networks benefit firms seeking financing. *American Sociological Review*, 481–505.

Walker, G., Kogut, B., & Shan, W. (1997). Social capital, structural holes and the formation of an industry network. *Organization Science*, *8*(2), 109–125.

Wasserman, S., & Faust, K. (1994). *Social network analysis: Methods and applications* (Vol. 8). Cambridge: Cambridge University Press.

Watts, D. J., & Strogatz, S. H. (1998). Collective dynamics of "small-world" networks. *Nature*, *393*(6684), 440.

Welser, H. T., Gleave, E., Fisher, D., & Smith, M. (2007). Visualizing the signatures of social roles in online discussion groups. *Journal of Social Structure*, *8*(2), 1–32.

Weterings, A., & Ponds, R. (2009). Do regional and non-regional knowledge flows differ? An empirical study on clustered firms in the Dutch life sciences and computing services industry. *Industry and Innovation*, *16*(1), 11–31.

Yeung, H. W. C. (2005). Rethinking relational economic geography. *Transactions of the Institute of British Geographers*, *30*(1), 37–51.

Yli-Renko, H., Autio, E., & Sapienza, H. J. (2001). Social capital, knowledge acquisition, and knowledge exploitation in young technology-based firms. *Strategic Management Journal*, *22*(6–7), 587–613.

Zaheer, A., & Bell, G. G. (2005). Benefiting from network position: Firm capabilities, structural holes, and performance. *Strategic Management Journal*, *26*(9), 809–825.

Zhao, L., & Aram, J. D. (1995). Networking and growth of young technology-intensive ventures in China. *Journal of Business Venturing*, *10*(5), 349–370.

3 Exploring the relational dimension of LIS

An empirical case study

3.1 A combined approach for the study of the LIS relational dimension

This chapter aims to explore the key concepts underpinning the relational dimension as a driver of LIS performance and illustrate the relative analytical challenges through the analysis of main contributions in the field. Based on reviewed studies in previous chapters, a lack of general agreement emerged about the optimal configuration of network structure with particular regard to its level of closure and openness. Furthermore, from a methodological perspective, most studies tend to limit their analyses to the observation of formal and inter-firm relationships, thus failing to highlight the variety of network portfolio and the heterogeneous actors' composition, which are two typical features of local innovation systems. In order to fill these gaps and in an attempt to capture both aspects of LIS's relational dimension (network structure and network portfolio composition), this chapter will explore:

(RQ1) Which is the configuration of the network structure in a successful local innovation system?

(RQ2) Which portfolio of relationships is implemented in a successful local innovation system?

In order to answer these questions, an exploratory, data-driven and qualitative-quantitative empirical case study of the biopharma LIS in Greater Boston Area is conducted. Case study research allows for the exploration and understanding of complex issues, and its robustness as a research strategy is particularly appreciated when an in-depth and holistic approach is required. Indeed, a case study approach allows examination of real-life situations, developing theories and assessing policies and programs and permits to give guidelines for strategic interventions (Soy, 1997; Baxter & Jack, 2008; Yin, 2009, 2015). More specifically, this research conducts an exploratory single case study. Compared to multiple or collective case studies, a single case study is more adequate when the case itself is either a representative or typical case, or a critical case as in the current study. Indeed, Yin (1994) proposed four strategies for case study selection according to the purpose of the case inquiry: the critical case, the extreme case, the unique case and the prelude case strategies. These strategies are used for testing, formulating or extending a theory, documenting a rare and unique case, investigating a phenomenon that is inaccessible to scientific research, and piloting a case in preparation for a multiple case design, respectively. In this book's case, a critical case study would allow for formulating propositions to be tested in future research, starting from the selection of a case study that meets all conditions that we are willing to explore. On the other hand, among all types of case study researches (explanatory, exploratory and descriptive), the exploratory case study is selected as it is particularly appropriate to research contexts that lack hypotheses (Yin, 2003), as in this case, and where the research environment limits the choice of methodology (Streb, 2010). In fact, exploratory case studies do not start with propositions and hypotheses deriving from prior literature review, but they rather develop descriptive analytic frameworks to redirect future empirical research (Hartley, 1994), as in this current study. Another aspect that is worth mentioning is that a case study design approach should not be confused with qualitative research, as it can indeed implement a mix of both qualitative and quantitative techniques. In fact, an important aim of the case study is capturing the complexity of a single case of study by integrating different levels of analysis, theoretical approaches and research techniques (Kohn, 1997; Johansson, 2003). This process is generally referred to as *triangulation*: a process where different methods and research techniques are combined to achieve a better validation of the study (Johansson, 2003). For this reason, a case study is generally referred to as a research strategy rather than a method (Kohlbacher, 2006).

The empirical case study in the current work is articulated in two phases:

- First, a network analytic study of strategic alliances and financial relationships among business, academic, corporate, start-up and government entities is developed.
- Second, a round of interviews with key stakeholders in the ecosystem is conducted in order to gain insights into the desirable network portfolio mix in terms of both strong and weak ties for the transfer of knowledge. The results of social network analysis (SNA) suggest insights about the optimal network structure (RQ1), as SNA has been widely used and has proven its efficacy for representing the features of the network structure configurations by providing visual and quantitative information on the level of openness and closure through a variety of specific indicators. However, the exclusive use of this methodology does not allow for capturing the whole variety of relationships occurring within an innovation ecosystem. More specifically, the relational data available in databases is usually indicators of formal relationships (financial, commercial and R&D). However, it is widely accepted that one of the main advantages deriving from geographical propinquity is the opportunity to exchange information through informal channels resulting from the establishment of personal relationships among co-located actors. These informal ties are generally excluded from quantitative relational data, and to overcome this limitation and gain insights about network portfolio, the SNA technique

is complemented with qualitative expert interviews. The conversations with key stakeholders allow for insights on the advantages of being in spatial proximity with partners and on the specific types of relationships that best contribute to knowledge transfer and to the innovation process (RQ2).

3.2 LIS in the biopharma industry

The term "biopharmaceutical" refers to the evolution of the pharmaceutical industry since its emergence in the late 1800s, when it was predominantly chemistry based, to include the more recent birth of biotechnology from the 1980s, which is based on living cells and molecules. More specifically, biotechnology refers to the whole set of technologies that employs and manipulates living cells and molecules with the aim of developing products and solutions that find their application in human health, agricultural production and other industries. As long as almost every pharmaceutical company is engaged in the development of biotech-related drugs, the distinction between *pharma* companies and *biotech* firms is increasingly less meaningful compared to past years. Nowadays, biopharmaceuticals cover about 20% of the whole pharmaceutical market and they represent its fastest growing branch. The present empirical study focuses on the process of biotech-based drug development, which consists of three main stages (Bianchi, Cavaliere, Chiaroni, Frattini, & Chiesa, 2011; Reynolds & Uygun, 2017) (Figure 3.1):

1 *Drug discovery*, including the following activities:

- *Target identification and validation*, which involves the selection of a gene or protein as a potential cause of a specific disease followed by a validation phase through the observation of data about the interactions of the target with human organisms. This stage requires a number of tools and procedures (e.g. cross-species studies, growing cell cultures, biomarkers for the measurement of biological functions).
- *Lead identification and optimization.* At this stage a new compound is developed with the aim of addressing the specific target identified in the previous steps and transformed in the active principle for the future drug through the addition of excipients.

2 *Drug development.* During this phase the drug has to undergo through a series of testing rounds, articulated in:

- *Pre-clinical tests*, where the new drug is initially tested on animals and subsequently subject to a first approval by public authorities before proceeding with the development.
- *Clinical tests*, which are articulated in Phase I, Phase II and Phase III. During these phases the drug is tested on human patients in order to validate the safety and to evaluate the efficacy of the new product. In case the response to these tests is positive, the new drug can be approved by public authorities to be commercialized in the market. In general, these first two stages (drug discovery and drug development) may take 10 to 15 years.

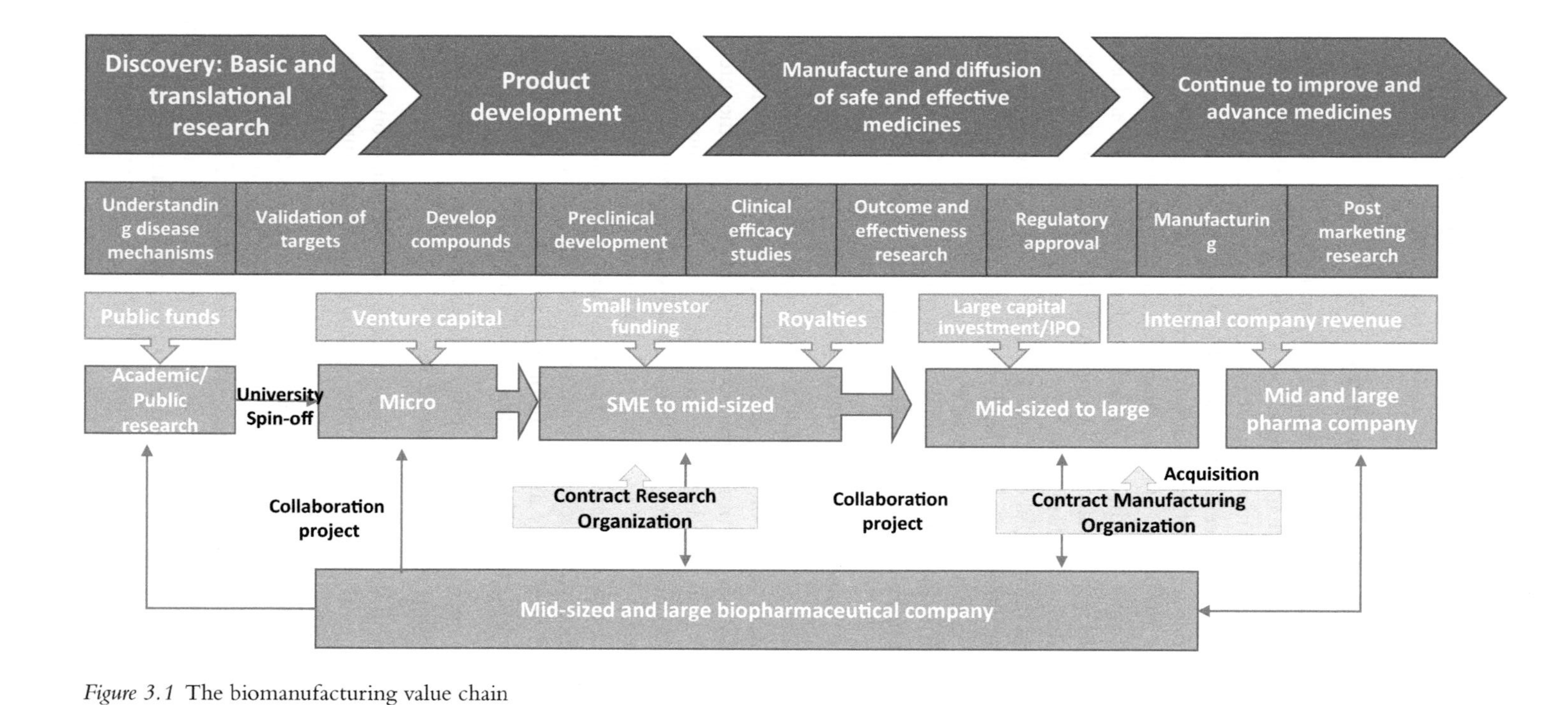

Figure 3.1 The biomanufacturing value chain

Source: Author's own elaboration from CRA (2014)

3 *Drug manufacturing at commercial scale.* During this phase a master cell line containing the gene to develop a specific protein is developed as well as a large number of cells to manufacture the protein. Afterwards, the protein is isolated and purified to be ready for patient use before being transferred in large bioreactors for scale-up. The *biomanufacturing* process is one of the most complex and riskiest industrial processes due to its high level of vulnerability to any slight change in the environment, which can potentially alter the drug quality and nullify its efficacy.

3.2.1 The importance of geographical proximity in the biopharma industry

The biopharmaceutical industry is characterized by a multidisciplinary structure that is typical of science-based sectors. One of its peculiarities is exemplified by the tendency of biopharmaceutical firms to cluster in a small number of geographical regions and to be significantly dependent on public research institutions for scientific capabilities and skilled labor (Audretsch & Stephan, 1996). Indeed, the industry is usually portrayed as a succession of highly specialized activities, each of which is in need of cooperation among private and public organizations. It has been argued that the development of a biopharma product requires the establishment of complex knowledge ecosystems (Reynolds, Zylberberg, & Del Campo, 2016) and following Owen-Smith and Powell (2004), geographic propinquity and network centrality represent two sources of competitive advantage for the industry's actors. Further explanation for the importance of relational capital and geographic proximity can be traceable to a number of reasons. First, the lengthy of the R&D life cycle requires a stable and supportive institutional environment. Second, the survival and the competitiveness of firms in biopharma sector are mainly based on continuous and technical innovation (Powell, Koput, & Smith-Doerr, 1996), which makes it crucial to gain access to new (and often tacit) knowledge and capabilities through both localized information spillovers as well as strategic alliances networks with a broader geographical scope. Finally, the high risks and costs associated to the R&D biopharma activities increase the dependence on risk capital, most notably public funds and venture capital. A recent study developed by Tufts University (Milne & Malins, 2012) estimates that the average cost for developing a biotech-based drug (from its early discovery to its commercialization) is approximately $2.6 billion (of which $1.4 billion is direct costs), which explains why the availability of risk capital providers is so important. Apart from the specific characteristics of the R&D activities, there are two broader factors that contribute to explain the key role of inter-organizational cooperation in the industry. One reason can be traceable to the fact that public-private collaborations have been further fostered by the enactment of the Bayh-Dole Act by the US Congress in 1980, which stimulated the emergence of new generation of academy-industry partnership models. The act stimulated the commercialization of government-funded research as it allowed universities and other non-profit entities to guard the property of patents resulting from research funded by federal grants. Indeed, prior to this university laboratories had served primarily as centers for basic biological research efforts without particular concern for commercial application. With reference to the biopharma industry, the Bayh-Dole Act created an environment that fostered partnerships for a rapid translation of scientific research into market-directed healthcare applications, thus increasing the innovation *appropriability* (Teece, 1986). Second, as emphasized by Ter Wal (2014), biotechnology industry has been interested by a shift in the technological regime from a predominantly generic to a more specialized knowledge base, known as the *second biotechnology revolution* (Gambardella, 1995). The advancements made in chemical engineering in the 1980s, driven by small biotech firms, brought a more rational approach to the development of new chemical substances and drug design. A large part of these firms, generally referred to as *dedicated biotech firms* (DBF), were originating from academic spin-offs and were highly specialized in biotechnology research and the realization of products with high commercial potential. However, their main limitation was the lack of resources required for clinical trials and strict bureaucratic approval procedures. Thus, from the mid-1980s big pharmaceutical companies began to provide financial support to DBFs for the development and commercialization of their products.

3.2.2 Demography of the biopharma industry

Before illustrating the portfolio of relationships typical of the biopharma industry, it is worth mentioning between whom these interactions occur. The industry is characterized by a heterogeneous demography where we can distinguish at least five different categories of stakeholders: dedicated biotechnology firms (DBFs), lead firms, contract manufacturing organizations (CMOs), contract research organizations (CROs) and public research organizations (PROs). DBFs usually originate as start-ups, founded by university-affiliated researchers with the aim of commercializing a specific technology or product resulting from research endeavors. As long as the skills required to bring a product to the market are too complex to be contained in a single firm (Powell et al., 1996), DBFs oftentimes rely on their relationships with competitors, domestic and international suppliers, public and private research institutions, technology transfer offices, universities, hospitals and public funding agencies to fill their knowledge gaps and fulfill those functions required for the development and exploitation of their product or technology (i.e. basic and applied research, clinical testing, marketing, regulatory engagement, distribution). Once they validate the early-stage efficacy of their drug, DBFs can take two alternative pathways of growth. On the one hand, these firms can initially seek for dilutive funding, by the means of a series of venture capital (VC) funds, and ultimately through an initial public offering (IPO). On the other hand, DBFs can be acquired by a large pharmaceutical or biopharmaceutical company.

However, due to the high rate of failure in the early phases of DBF development, their capability of bearing the risks related to drug development may be hindered. In fact, it is generally after the achievement of a certain level of initial success that DBFs can raise their expectations about their rapid growth through VC or acquisition. Lead firms are large pharmaceutical or biopharmaceutical companies that often undertake a facilitator role in the management of networks of biotechnology start-ups, university laboratories and international suppliers to bring a drug to the market. CMOs, also referred to as contract development and manufacturing organizations (CDMOs), are firms that provide a set of services ranging from drug development to drug manufacturing on a contract basis. Main services include pre-clinical and Phase I clinical trial materials, late-stage clinical trial materials, registration batches and commercial production. Their proliferation is in line with the pharmaceutical companies' tendency to outsource a part of R&D operations to focus most of their efforts on drug discovery and marketing, thus expanding their technical resources without excessively increased overhead costs. Similarly, CROs are engaged in bioassay development, pre-clinical and clinical research, clinical trials management (patient recruitment and data collection) and drug safety testing. Their main function is indeed that of supporting large firms in meeting the complex regulatory pathway underpinning drug development and commercialization. PROs are universities and non-profit institutes that are engaged in research that is valuable to industry. These are deemed to play a key role in knowledge production on a research frontier and they allow for a pursuit of more open technological trajectories as they, compared to for-profit organizations, create different selection environments for early-stage research. The biopharma ecosystem demography is also characterized by the presence of VC firms and public agencies that undertake the role of capital risk providers as well as that of facilitator and business support, as will be illustrated in the empirical case in the following sections.

3.2.3 Forms of collaboration in the biopharma industry

The practices of cooperation within biopharma ecosystems occur during the whole innovation pipeline and present different degrees of formalization depending on their scope. In this section the main forms of inter-organizational relationships are illustrated. Some of them are typical of most industries while others are more specific to the biopharma sector. One of the most traditional forms of innovation-driven cooperation occurs through partnering in *R&D strategic alliances*. This refers to the development of research programs through a formal relationship between two or more parties to pursue a set of agreed-upon goals, while remaining independent organizations, for a specific target where all parties contribute in a joint endeavor. Generally, it is based on the complementarity of the skills and assets between the partners involved. Similarly, co-patenting refers to relationships established through the co-development and co-ownership of patents by universities and other organizations. Another common practice is *sponsored research*. In this case, it is common that large firms fund a program of R&D that is developed entirely or mostly by an academic research group or a smaller company. Depending on the degree of engagement of the funding organization, this type of relationship may follow a *fee-for-service* model, where the commissioner presents a more hands-off approach. *Joint clinical trials*, which generally involve academic medical centers, DBFs and big pharmaceutical companies represent another typical practice of cooperation in biopharma. This regards the cooperation in conducting trials of products on subjects for US Food and Drug Administration (FDA) approval (Powell et al., 1996). *IP transfer* represents a widespread practice in the biotech industry. Indeed, it is frequent for small biotech firms and academic research groups working on innovative approaches to act as technology providers throughout licensing agreements with the aim of monetizing a certain innovation that can potentially become the seed of a drug discovery or solve a technical problem in an existing large company's ongoing project. The frequency of the interaction between the licensee and licensor usually varies according to the degree of the originator's involvement in actively monitoring and controlling the use of the IP as well as providing support and guidance for its implementation. The issues pertaining to the appropriability of the developed innovation also underpins the *spin-off generation* (i.e. the creation of a separate company from part of an existing firm). This is considered a form of relation due to the high level of interaction with the originator-organization. Following the increasing specialization that characterizes R&D activities in the field and the level of inter-organizational competitiveness, we have witnessed the proliferation of the so-called *value added supply agreements*. It is a common practice for biopharma organizations to outsource specific non-core R&D operations (e.g. clinical data monitoring, chemical reference compound synthesis), typically to CROs. While many of these are highly standardized practices that do not require a high level of interaction and are regarded as usual buyer-seller transactions, there is a significant number of supplier arrangements that become real partnerships, with a close integration of operations and benefits in terms of cost and time savings for the customer. The reasons of establishing collaborative supply arrangements may be traceable to the high level of customization that requires the customer's participation to the delivery of the process. VC and other private capital (such as business angel seed investment or corporate venture capital [CVC]) have been key to fostering start-ups in the biopharmaceutical industry due to the high costs and risks of the industry R&D process. Traditional VC and CVC can assume multiple forms ranging from funding to transformative technologies with the potential to be turned into a variety of products to investing exclusively in existing companies in return of equity. Finally, a more traditional form of inter-organization cooperation is the *joint venture*, which is common across diverse industries and envisages the constitution of a third independent organization as a result of the joint effort of two or more parties with a shared vision and goals. The types of partnerships illustrated above mainly exemplify forms of formal and contractual relationships that tend to be strong and long-term. However, it has been widely recognized the high potential for innovation resulting from less formal types of interactions. As a way of illustration, *interlocking directorates* represent an informal channel of information exchange as this practice refers to the presence of the same person in the boards of directors of two or more organizations. Also, there is a growing interest in the establishment of formal and informal agreements for the *mobility of human resources* among industry and university through internship programs and targeted job placement policies. Another common practice in the industry is exemplified by the *agreements for the access and use of infrastructure*, which provide access to infrastructure and facilities in an innovation center to allow or facilitate the exercise of certain research activities for both companies and research groups often governed by contracts, for example, membership in incubators, that are areas of services designed to accommodate new businesses that can benefit of the shared use of expensive equipment as well as cheap office space and business consultancy services. Finally, the *co-participation to thematic associations or consortia* is a newer form of collaboration regarded as a burgeoning area of partnerships. The association or the consortium may bring together resources, direct research pathways and gather experts from the industry with the aim of enabling a specific research endeavor that could not be undertaken by a single organization alone. A more complete list of the most implemented practices of inter-organizational relationships is provided in Table 3.1.

3.3 The biopharma innovation system in the Greater Boston Area

This empirical study is conducted in the case of the Greater Boston Area (GBA) biopharma system. Due to its high-ranking position among US biotech clusters (JJL U.S. Life Science, 2016), the GBA is considered a benchmark case for LIS successful performance. The GBA is renowned as the leading US life science cluster (JJL U.S. Life Science, 2016) for the amount of patent ownership per capita, VC funding and number of IPOs. The region is home to many leaders in technology and life science as well as world-class academic and research institutions as Harvard University and the Massachusetts Institute of Technology (MIT). The area hosts approximately 250,000 students across 52 higher education institutions and can rely on the largest concentration of life science researchers in the country as well as world-class medical facilities, including the top three hospitals funded by the National Institutes of Health (NIH). As a result of direct access to top talent, the GBA has attracted a dynamic community of investors. More precisely, VC funding is $2.58 billion, which represents 38% of the total VC funding of the US, which in turn makes the GBA particularly attractive to innovative entrepreneurs. The life science industry in the area employs more than 86,000 individuals with an average annual employment growth rate of 1.3% (Table 3.2). As a result, 22,000 new jobs have been created in the area, only in the last ten years.

Table 3.1 Practices of inter-organizational relationships

	Definition	*Type of tie*	*Partners*	*Source*
Strategic R&D partnerships	Development of research programs with other organizations for a specific target to pursue a set of agreed-upon goals while remaining independent organizations	Formal	DBFs, pharmaceutical corporations, research institutes and university labs	Powell et al. (1996) and Owen-Smith and Powell (2004)
IP transfer	In-licensing and out-licensing agreements to commercialize the results of scientific efforts or purchase rights to partner's idea	Formal	DBFs, pharmaceutical corporations, research institutes and university labs	Ensing (2017), Powell et al. (1996), Owen-Smith and Powell (2005) and Bianchi et al. (2011)
Sponsored research	Large organizations fund an R&D program that is developed entirely or mostly by research institutions	Formal	Pharmaceutical corporations, research institutes and university labs	Ensing (2017)
Joint clinical trials	DBF has partner conduct trials of products on subject for FDA approval	Formal	Research hospitals and firms specializing in clinical hospitals	Powell et al. (1996) and Owen-Smith and Powell (2005)
Value added supply agreements	Outsourcing of non-core R&D activities based on long-term and highly customized agreements	Formal	Large chemical or pharmaceutical corporations, CROs and CMOs	Powell et al. (1996), Owen-Smith and Powell (2005), Kajiwata (2010), Capello and Faggian (2005) and Ensing (2017)
Joint venture	DBF invests funds (and usually human/scientific capital) in a partner	Formal	Other biotech firms	Powell et al. (1996) and Owen-Smith and Powell (2005)
VC and seed funds	Seed capital and investment relations in return of equity	Formal	Start-ups, business angels and VC firms	Still, Huhtamäki, Russell and Rubens (2014) Powell et al. (1996) and Owen-Smith and Powell (2005)

Spin-offs	The creation of a separate company from part of an existing firm	Formal	Universities, public institutions and corporations	Capello and Faggian (2005)
Agreements for the access to infrastructure	Provide access to infrastructures in an innovative center to allow or facilitate the exercise of certain research activities for both companies and research groups often governed by contracts (e.g. incubator: areas of services designed to accommodate new businesses)	Formal	Large chemical or pharmaceutical corporations, research institutes and university labs	Ter Wal (2014)
Co-patenting	Relationships established through the co-development and co-ownership of patents by universities and other organizations	Formal	DBFs, pharmaceutical corporations, research institutes and university labs	Capellari et al. (2016)
Mobility of human resource between different organizations through formal or informal agreements	In the transition to a new organization, a manager/researcher could maintain relations with the organization of origin subject; even in the absence of relationships, the subject brings with it knowledge and experience in another context	Informal/ formal	Corporations and research institutes	Simoni and Schiavone (2009) and Capello and Faggian (2005)
Interlocking directorates	The presence of the same person in the respective boards of directors	Informal	Corporations, universities and research institutes	Mizruchi (1992) and Davis et al. (2003)
Co-participation to thematic associations	The consortium brings together resources, direct research pathways and gather experts from the industry with the aim of enabling a specific research endeavor that could not be taken by a single organization alone	Informal	Corporations, universities and research institutes	Milne and Malins (2012)

Source: Author's own elaboration

Table 3.2 The biopharma LIS in the Greater Boston Area: economic scorecard

Workforce	*Total life science*	*% life science to private employment*	*Year-over-year growth*
Employment	86,235	4.5%	1.3%
Establishments	2,136	4.3%	12.7%
Funding	**Total life science**	**% of total US**	
VC funding	$2.580 billion	38.01%	
NIH funding	$2.057 billion	18.72%	

Source: Author's own elaboration from JJL U.S. Life Science (2016)

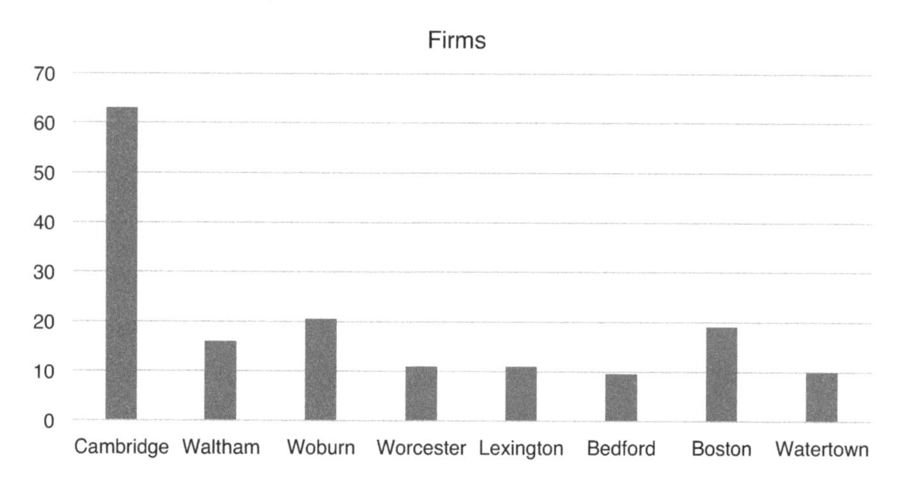

Figure 3.2 The biopharma LIS in the Greater Boston Area: biotechnology firms by city

Source: Author's own elaboration from Breznitz (2015)

The city of Cambridge is one of the most competitive global centers in the life science industry. East Cambridge alone is home to 87.4% of the city's lab space (JJL U.S. Life Science, 2016) and hosts 30% of GBA firms and 60% of the employment (Breznitz, 2015) (Figures 3.2 and 3.3).

Even in the city of Cambridge there is a high level of local clustering, with specific regard to Kendall Square, a 10-acre area located in East Cambridge across the Charles River from Massachusetts General Hospital and adjacent to the MIT campus, comprising a business district that hosts a number of global technology firms such as Amazon, Google, Facebook and Microsoft, as well as the biggest world players in the biopharma industry including Novartis, Genzyme, Lilly, Abbvie and Biogen, among others (Figure 3.4). Kendall Square in Cambridge has been defined as "the most innovative square mile on the planet", with regard to the high concentration of entrepreneurial start-ups

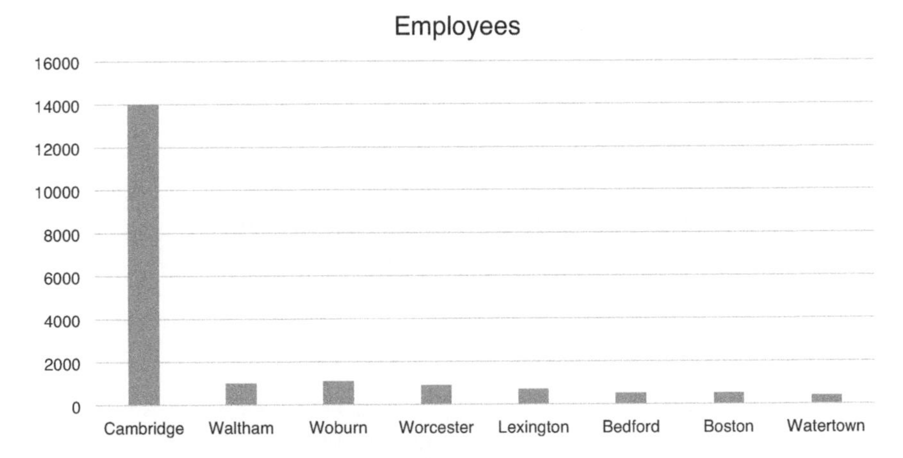

Figure 3.3 The biopharma LIS in the Greater Boston Area: biotechnology by employment

Source: Author's own elaboration from Breznitz (2015)

and the quality of innovation that has emerged in the proximity of the square since 2010. The rise of life science in Kendall Square was accompanied by the parallel decline in Boston's earlier innovation area district for technology, known as Route 128. This is the area in north Boston that had been competing with Silicon Valley as a technology center thanks to its booming minicomputer and mainframe industry, partly fueled by military sector funds. As highlighted by Saxenian (1996), Route 128 was unable to compete due to a vertical network structure dominated by a few large firms resulting in a closed model of innovation that failed to exploit the external sources of novelty as Silicon Valley did. In the early 21st century, the MIT Investment Company (MITIMCo) focused its expansion plans toward the Kendall Square area. One of the emblematic outcomes of this strategy is represented by One Broadway Center, where a significant number of high-performing companies and organizations reside, including the popular Cambridge Innovation Center (CIC), a co-working space on the 14th floor that provides start-ups (especially biotech) with a place to convene, work and grow. Similar to CIC, LabCentral, created in 1999, now represents another example of facilities for small biotech businesses that offer lab space and resources to scale and foster innovative ideas. By 2010 Kendall Square had turned into the focal point of the GBA innovation system. However, a few pitfalls followed its expansion. More specifically, the expensive real estate market makes it difficult for start-ups to survive in the area. As a consequence, many companies have started to relocate in different areas. The Seaport District and the core suburbs (Lexington, Waltham, Worcester and Bedford) have become attractive to mid-size tenants as well as more established companies due to their more affordable real estate market.

Figure 3.4 Kendall Square, Cambridge, Massachusetts

Source: http://maps.google.com

By way of illustration, in 2014 Vertex Pharmaceutical relocated from East Cambridge to the Seaport District.

3.4 Methodology

3.4.1 The social network analysis

SNA has been widely implemented for the sociological study of individuals and organizations (Wasserman & Faust, 1994; Welser, Gleave, Fisher, & Smith, 2007) as well as for the assessment of nested structures of inter-firm relationships (Moody & White, 2003; Halinen, 2012). Networks' main components are actors (nodes or vertexes) and their ties (edges or links). Ties are either directed, in those cases in which the arrows provide "from-to" information, or undirected. The complete set of nodes and ties is generally referred to as the *social graph*, or simply the graph. In graph theory's basic terminology, the number of ties that a node has is its degree, which can be further distinguished by *in-degree* and *out-degree.* The sequence of ties and nodes between one another and another is a *path*, and *path length* indicates the number of degrees between two nodes, often referred to as the *distance* between two nodes. Visual network analysis can serve as a tool for revealing the flow of information, know-how and financial resources among different actors (Russell, Still, Huhtamäki, Yu, & Rubens, 2011). Relational metrics can allow for a deeper understanding of system's emergent structures, patterns and transformation dynamics (Freeman, 2002) and allow for a comparative analysis over time and across regions. As analyzed in Chapter 2, a number of authors have employed network metrics as indicators of relational capital to explore the structure of innovation ecosystems. The metrics for understanding the dynamics of an innovation system are distinguished based on the distinct yet related levels of analysis: the network as a whole (ecosystem) and the node level (firm/individual; Basole, Clear, Hu, Mehrotra, & Stasko, 2013). Accordingly, network metrics can be divided in two broad groups:

- *Centrality metrics*, which consider positions of individuals in the network;
- *Structural metrics*, which consider the whole network and its components.

At the organizational and the individual level, centrality metrics generally indicate the number of connections, the frequency of occurrence on paths between others and the diversity of connections. These indicators are usually used to identify those nodes that are well positioned to influence the network or to channel information. Some of the most common indicators are *node degree centrality* and *betweenness centrality*, which are calculated for understanding the functions of individual nodes or, in other words, of the actors in the ecosystem. In particular, node degree centrality exemplifies the number of connections for a given vertex, providing information on its immediate connectivity and popularity and influence in the networks. A node's in-degree or out-degree is the number of links that lead into or out of the node, and in an undirected graph they are obviously identical. The *closeness centrality* calculates the mean length of all shortest paths from a vertex to all the other ones in the network. It is a measure of reach in the sense that it indicates the speed with which information can reach other nodes from a given starting vertex. Betweenness centrality indicates the number of times that a given node appears in the shortest path from all nodes in the network to all others. As a consequence, betweenness centrality shows the importance of a node in bridging the different parts or components of the network together. High betweenness centrality means that a node has a bridging role between different parts of the overall network. The *average betweenness centrality* shows the availability of bridging relationships across the system. Finally, a node's *eigenvector centrality* is proportional to the sum of the eigenvector centralities of all nodes directly connected to it. Put differently, a node with a high eigenvector centrality is linked to other nodes with high eigenvector centrality. At the meso-structural level, some of the most common indicators are *modularity*, which is the fraction of links that fall within modules minus the expected value of the same quantity if the links fall at random without regard for the modular structure; and *within-module degree*, which indicates how the node is positioned, thus measuring how "well connected" the node is to other nodes in the module. At the structural level, most common indicators include the *density* of interactions, the *average degree* of separation and cross-group or cross-organization *connectivity*. These measures are particularly useful for comparing groups within networks or for gaining insights about changes in a network over time. The profile of the ecosystem is generally described through indicators of *size* and *composition* of the network. While the size is usually represented through the number of nodes and edges, the composition refers to the concept of homophily, which is the tendency to relate to nodes with similar characteristics that, in turn, leads to the formation of homogeneous groups (clusters), where establishing relations is deemed to be easier. Another aspect that can be measured through SNA structural indicators is the level of engagement of network's actors, usually indicated through the *ratio of edge to node* (i.e. the number of connections between nodes in the ecosystem). Additionally, a network's density, which is usually referred to as an indicator of vitality, is the ratio of the number of edges in the network over the total number of possible edges between all pairs of nodes (which is $n(n-1)/2$, where n is the number of vertices, for an undirected graph); it is a common measure of how tightly connected a network is. A perfectly connected network is called a *clique* and has density equal to 1. Conversely, a directed graph will present half the density of its undirected equivalent, as there are twice as many possible edges: $n(n-1)$. Density is particularly useful in comparing networks against each other or in doing the same for different regions within a single network. Two other common indicators, which are often referred to as *small world properties*, are the *average clustering coefficient* and the *average path length*. A node's clustering coefficient is the number of closed triplets in the node's neighborhood over the total number of triplets in the neighborhood, also known as *transitivity*. Clustering algorithms detect clusters or "groups" within networks on the basis of network structure and specific clustering criteria. While analyzing the structure of a network, the main indicator is the average clustering coefficient, which shows the ecosystem's overall connectivity based on local relationships. The average path length is the average graph distance between all pairs of nodes. The longest shortest path (distance) between any two nodes is known as the *network's diameter*, which is a useful indicator of the reach of the network (instead of focusing only on the total number of nodes or edges). It also provides information about how long it will take at most to reach any vertex in the network (sparser networks usually present greater diameters). Additionally, the average path length (average of all shortest paths) in a network is an interesting indicator of how far apart any two vertexes are expected to be on average (average distance). As further indicators of cohesion, it is possible to compute the *size of the major component* (i.e. the percentage of nodes belonging to the main component), which shows the cohesion to belonging to the largest group of the ecosystem, and the *ratio of the number of relations*, in which there is an edge in both directions over the total number of relations in the network. This is a useful indicator of the degree of mutuality and reciprocal exchange in a network, which relate to social cohesion, but it only makes sense in directed graphs (Table 3.3).

3.4.2 Expert interviews

The expert interview is a consolidated methodology of qualitative empirical research, designed to explore expert knowledge, which has increased its popularity since the early 1990s. More specifically, expert interview has found increasing application in social science and its modes of implementation, from its role in individual research design to the methods used to decode and analyze its results, varies on a case basis. This method has been increasingly applied also for the study of innovation-driven networks (see e.g. Bianchi et al., 2011). However, it is widely accepted that the popularity gained by this methodology is due to the fact that, in relative terms, talking to experts during the exploratory phase of research projects turns out to be a more efficient and concentrated way to gather data compared to, for example, systematic quantitative surveys or participatory observation. Indeed, expert interviews can contribute to shorten the lengthy data gathering processes, especially in case of experts who are considered as "crystallization points" for achieving insider knowledge from practitioners and regarded as surrogates for a wider circle of stakeholders. One of the main methodological concerns that researchers are faced with is the identification of the "experts". Meuser and Nagel (1991) provide one of the most accredited definitions of expert, regarded as either a "Person who is responsible for the development, implementation or control of solutions/strategies/policies" or a "Person who has privileged access to information about groups of persons or decision processes" (De Bruijn-Geraets, Van Eijk-Hustings, & Vrijhoef, 2014, p. 2678). Expert interviews can be used for different purposes. In this regard, Bogner and Menz (2002) provide a topology of expert interviews on the basis of the different purposes they are used for. Primarily, expert interviews can be

Table 3.3 The most common indicators in social network analysis

		Snapshot indicator	*Description*
Structural	Types of actors present	The similarity of actors present (homophily/heterophily)	The composition of the ecosystem
	Quantity of actors and ties	Number of nodes	Ratio of edge to node: the number of connections between nodes in the ecosystem
		Number of edges	
	Diameter	The longest shortest path (distance) between any two nodes	Indicator of the reach of the network (sparser networks usually present greater diameters)
	Density	Represents how tightly the network is connected	The actual interconnectedness in the ecosystem's overall connectivity based on local relationships (the actual edges divided by the potential edges)
	Clustering coefficient	The level of connectivity between the directly connected partners	Average clustering coefficient: showing the ecosystem's overall connectivity based on local relationships
	Average path length	Indicator of how far apart any two vertexes are expected to be on average (average distance)	The average graph distance between all pairs of nodes
	Major component	Size of the main component	Percentage of nodes showing the cohesion to belonging to the largest group of the ecosystem
		Percentage of nodes belonging to the main component	
	Degree of reciprocity	Indicator of the degree of mutuality and reciprocal exchange in a network (only in directed graphs)	The ratio of the number of relations in which there is an edge in both directions, over the total number of relations in the network

Meso-structural	Modularity	Measures the strength of division of a network into modules (or groups, clusters or communities). Networks with high modularity have dense connections between the nodes within modules but sparse connections between nodes in different modules. It is used for detecting *community structure* in networks.	The fraction of links that fall within modules, minus the expected value of the same quantity
	Within-module degree (z-score)	Indicates how "well connected" the node is to other nodes in the module	Intramodule z-scored within the node's module
Organization and individual	Node degree of centrality	Provides information on node's immediate connectivity and popularity and influence in the networks	The number of available connections In-degree (the number of incoming connections) Out-degree (the number of outgoing connections)
	Betweenness centrality	High betweenness centrality means that a node has a connecting role as a bridge between the different parts of the overall network	Average betweenness centrality: showing the availability of bridging relationships across the system
	Closeness centrality	A measure of reach as it indicates the speed with which information can reach other nodes from a given starting vertex	The mean length of all shortest paths from a vertex to all the other ones in the network
	Eigenvector centrality	A node with a high eigenvector centrality is linked to other nodes with high eigenvector centrality	A node's eigenvector centrality is proportional to the sum of the eigenvector centralities of all nodes directly connected to it

Source: Author's own elaboration

used for exploring a new field of study to find topical patterns and to develop research hypotheses. Second, this methodology can be implemented for collecting contextual information to complementary findings deriving from the application of other methodologies. Finally, expert interviews may be applied for theory building by developing a framework as a result of knowledge reconstruction from various experts. For the development of the empirical study of this thesis, the second typology of expert interview was implemented (the *systematizing expert interview*) to complement results deriving from the social network analysis. Interviews as a qualitative research methodology may take different forms (i.e. semi-structured, structured and unstructured). This study conducts semi-structured in-depth interviews which, differently from structured interviews that present only closed questions, are conducted with a fairly open framework that allows for focused, conversational, two-way communication where respondents have to answer open-ended questions for the duration of 30 minutes to more than an hour. More specifically, these are based on an *interview guide* (i.e. a schematic presentation of questions or topics to be explored by the interviewer). The interview guide consists of core questions as well as a number of associated questions that may improve further through pilot testing of the interview guide. The interview guide allows the researcher to achieve a more systematic and efficient exploration as it contributes to keeping the conversation focused on the desired line of action. The main advantage of semi-structured, in-depth interviews lies in the combination of both structure and flexibility, which allows respondents to interact with the investigator in terms of the issue under research, thus providing much more detailed information compared to other techniques to gather data, such as surveys, especially in those cases when an interviewee's answer to a preset question raises issues that the interview may further explore through follow-up questions. This specific interview format is particularly appropriate in those cases in which there is a limited sample of key interviewees whose expertise and experience in the field under investigation may raise issues not previously covered by the researcher, allowing for a thicker understanding of the field (Corbin & Strauss, 2008; Gray, 2009; Corbin & Morse, 2003).

3.4.3 Data collection and analysis for SNA

To explore data-driven network analytics by taking into account the diversity of the LIS community, I selected the sample based on their memberships to MassBio, the freely available membership directory of the Massachusetts Biotechnology Council. MassBio counts more than 975 members dedicated to advancing cutting-edge research in the life science industry in Massachusetts and provides information on their location, typology and area of specialization. Members range from academic hospitals and non-profit organizations to pharmaceutical biotech companies and capital providers. I selected those organizations with headquarters or branch offices having mailing addresses in the metropolitan areas of Greater Boston. The spatial identification of each area included the suburban city names associated with identification of those cities having more than 50,000

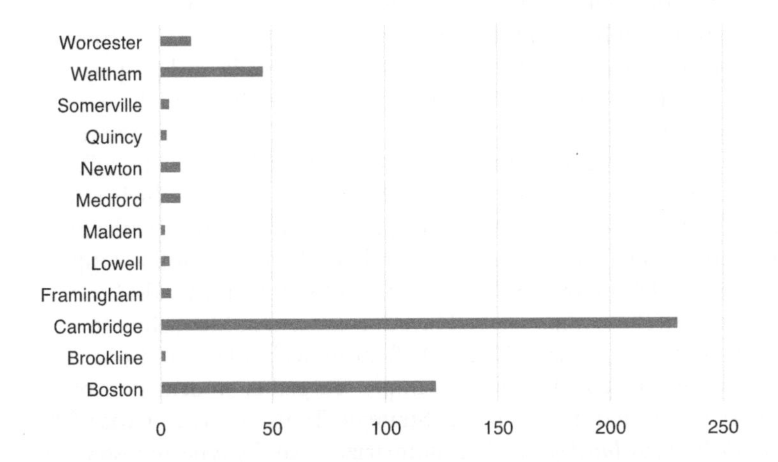

Figure 3.5 Geographical distribution: MassBio members in GBA (2012–2017)

Source: Author's own elaboration from MassBio

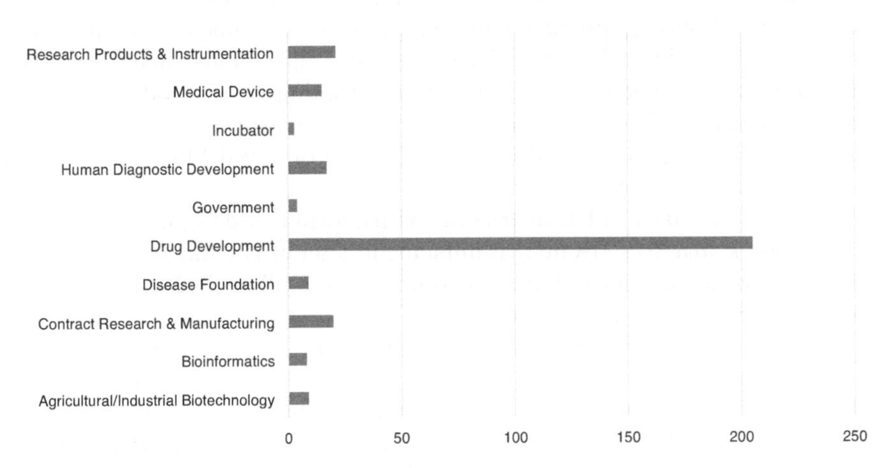

Figure 3.6 Areas of specialization: MassBio members in GBA (2012–2017)

Source: Author's own elaboration from MassBio

inhabitants (U.S. Census Bureau, 2015) (Figure 3.5). Additionally, included in the sample are only those members belonging to the biopharma industry that specialize in drug development (Figure 3.6). The final sample counts 444 organizations distributed as follows: 85 academic hospitals and non-profit organizations (universities, research institutes, hospitals, government agencies, incubators); 55 capital risk providers (VC, CVC, hedge funds, private equity (PE) firms); and 304 pharma-biotech firms (big pharmas, DBFs, CROs, start-ups).

To reveal insights about the overall innovation system's structure of the GBA, this study regards two types of relationships: first, financial transactions represented by *venture deals* (i.e. Series A-E/Round 1–5, grant, seed, private investment in public equity (PIPE), add-on, venture debt) and *strategic alliances* (i.e. R&D and marketing-licensing, purchase of intellectual property, spin-out, spin-off, trial collaboration, reverse licensing, product purchase, product or technology swap, joint venture, intra biotech deals). To create the final dataset, I relied on two sources of relational data about relationships. To collect data on venture deals, I used Preqin Dataset (Preqin Ltd., 2017), which is a comprehensive and historical database on the private equity industry offering detailed information and analytics on firms, funds, deals and portfolio companies dating back to 1999 on over 5,000 funds and 11,000 hedge funds. I selected deals between portfolio companies and investors located in Massachusetts completed within the last five years (2012–2017) in biotechnology and pharmaceutical industries and matched with our sample. To gather information on strategic alliances I collected data from the Strategic Transactions Database (*Pharma & MedTech Business Intelligence*) that summarizes deals by type, industry and sector from 1995 to date. I collected information on strategic alliances initiated or completed within the 2012–2017 time frame including R&D and marketing-licensing, purchase of intellectual property, spin-out, spin-off, trial collaboration, reverse licensing, product purchase, product or technology swap, joint venture and intra biotech deals and matched our sample. I integrated these two databases into a single dataset on networks consisting of 450 nodes and 289 links. The links are non-directed in order to measure small world properties (Kajikawa, Takeda, Sakata, & Matsushima, 2010). I observed 148 venture deals and 141 strategic alliances (Table 3.4).

To present the data and its metrics in a visual form I used Gephi, an interactive network analysis software that implements a set of key functionalities for visual network analytics and metrics computation (Still et al., 2014). I used a force-driven algorithm where nodes repel each other and edges pull the connected nodes together to gain insights on the spatial structure of relationships (Russell, Huhtamäki, Still, Rubens, & Basole, 2015). In graph theory, force-driven layout reveals the macro-level structure of the network including the key clusters and the key brokers in the network, as well as possible structural holes (Burt, 1992). I also provided complementary network visualization by using Kumu, a data visualization platform to organize complex information into interactive relationship maps (www.kumu.io). In the first visualization (Gephi), color-coding was added to provide information about the frequency of the tie (measured by counting the number of interaction in the time frame). In the second case (Kumu), color-coding was included to differentiate the types of edges. Tie data allowed me to calculate measures of network structure that I used to evaluate the level of *embeddedness* of the network and to classify individual ties by their type: (1) R&D partnerships (i.e. R&D strategic alliances and clinical trials), (2) venture deals, (3) joint ventures, (4) IP transfer (which includes licensing agreements, product purchase, technology swap and acquisition of intellectual property rights), (5) spin-off/spin-out and (6) other biotech deals.

Table 3.4 Data sources

	Preqin Dataset (Preqin Ltd. 2017)	*Strategic Transactions Database* (Pharma & MedTech Business Intelligence)
Source of data	Comprehensive and historical data on the private equity industry offering detailed information and analytics on firms, funds, deals and portfolio companies dating back to 1999 on over 5,000 funds and 11,000 hedge funds	Summaries of deals by type, industry and sector, 1995 to date
Ecosystem entities	Big pharmas, biotech firms, start-ups and risk capital providers	Big pharmas, biotech firms, start-ups, risk capital providers and academic, hospital and non-profit institutions
Types of relationships	Venture deals (148) between firms and investors co-located in the GBA	Strategic alliances (141) R&D and marketing-licensing, purchase of intellectual property, spin-out, spin-off, trial collaboration, reverse licensing, product purchase, product or technology swap, joint venture, intra biotech deals, marketing-licensing

Source: Author's own elaboration

3.4.4 Data collection and analysis for expert interviews

In order to gain insights about the most desirable network portfolio mix a round of expert interviews was organized and carried out with nine key informants who have been chosen as representatives of the different categories of stakeholders in the biopharma ecosystem of the GBA. The interviews were conducted directly by the author. The list of participants who took part in each interview is reported in Table 3.5 and the profiles of the represented organizations are illustrated in Table 3.6. I assumed that the conditions that distinguish LIS from other forms of territorial aggregations (e.g. industrial districts) and aspatial innovation systems (e.g. technological/sectorial systems of innovation) are:

- The existence of knowledge-intensive relationships for the combination of non-existing knowledge (analytic base of knowledge), and
- The embeddedness of the LIS' actors found in spatial proximity, which in turns allows for easier access to information.

(Ferretti & Parmentola, 2015)

Table 3.5 Expert interviews: represented organizations

Organization	Description
MIT Department of Chemical Engineering	Formally established as a separate department in 1920, MIT's Chemical Engineering department (ChemE) has not only set the standard for instruction and research in the field, it continues to redefine the discipline's frontiers. With one of three undergraduate programs focusing on chemical-biological engineering for students interested in the emerging biotech and life sciences industries, and two of three graduate programs providing an experiential course of study in chemical engineering practice in collaboration with MIT's Sloan School of Management, ChemE at MIT is quite unlike chemical engineering anywhere else. In 2017, for the 29th consecutive year, *US News & World Report* gave its top rankings to both ChemE's graduate and undergraduate programs among US chemical engineering departments. In 2017, for the 7th straight year, MIT Chemical Engineering has been ranked first in the world by QS World University Rankings. More than 10% of the alumni are senior executives of industrial companies. Nearly 25% of the recipients of major awards presented by the American Institute of Chemical Engineers and the American Chemical Society's Murphree Award have been alumni or faculty of MIT. *Source:* https://cheme.mit.edu
Massachusetts Life Science Center (MLSC)	The Massachusetts Life Sciences Center (MLSC) is an investment agency that supports life sciences innovation, education, research and development, and commercialization. The MLSC is charged with implementing a $1-billion, state-funded investment initiative to create jobs and support advances that improve health and well-being. The MLSC offers the nation's most comprehensive set of incentives and collaborative programs targeted to the life sciences ecosystem. These programs propel the growth that has made Massachusetts the global leader in life sciences. The MLSC creates new models for collaboration and partners with organizations, both public and private, around the world to promote innovation in the life sciences. *Source:* www.masslifesciences.com
Novartis	Novartis is a Swiss multinational pharmaceutical company based in Basel, Switzerland. It is one of the largest pharmaceutical companies by both market capital and sales. Novartis manufactures the drugs clozapine (Clozaril), diclofenac (Voltaren), carbamazepine (Tegretol), valsartan (Diovan) and imatinib mesylate (Gleevec/Glivec). Additional agents include ciclosporin (Neoral/Sandimmune), letrozole (Femara), methylphenidate (Ritalin), terbinafine (Lamisil), and others. *Source:* www.novartis.com
Ironwood Pharmaceuticals, Inc.	Ironwood Pharmaceuticals, Inc. is a biotechnology company. The Company is advancing product opportunities in areas of unmet needs, including irritable bowel syndrome with constipation (IBS C), and chronic idiopathic constipation (CIC), hyperuricemia associated with uncontrolled gout, uncontrolled gastroesophageal reflux disease (uncontrolled GERD), and vascular and fibrotic diseases. It operates in human therapeutics business segment. Its product, linaclotide, is available to adult men and women suffering from IBS C or CIC in the United States under the trademarked name Linzess, and is available to adult men and women suffering from IBS C in certain European countries under the trademarked name Constella. It is also advancing IW-3718, a gastric retentive formulation of a bile acid sequestrant with the potential to provide symptomatic relief in patients with uncontrolled GERD. Its vascular/fibrotic programs include IW-1973 and IW-1701, which targets soluble guanylate cyclase (sGC). *Source:* www.ironwoodpharma.com

Alnylam	Alnylam is leading the translation of RNA interference (RNAi) into a whole new class of innovative medicines with the potential to transform the lives of patients who have limited or inadequate treatment options. Based on Nobel Prize-winning science, RNAi therapeutics represent a powerful, clinically validated approach for the treatment of a wide range of debilitating diseases with high unmet medical need. Alnylam was founded in 2002 on a bold vision to turn scientific possibility into reality, which is now marked by its robust discovery platform and deep pipeline of investigational medicines, including 4 programs in late-stage clinical development. *Source:* www.alnylam.com
Obsidian Therapeutics	Obsidian Therapeutics, founded by Atlas Venture in 2016, is a biotech firm based in Cambridge, which develops next-generation cell and gene therapeutics that employ precise exogenous control of transgenes for improved safety and efficacy. *Source:* https://obsidiantx.com/
Angiex	Angiex was founded is a start-up biotech firm that develops vascular-targeted biotherapeutics. Angiex targets fundamental aspects of endothelial biology with a focus on angiogenesis; its lead product is an antibody-drug conjugate therapy for cancer. Angiex was launched with IP from Beth Israel Deaconess Medical Center, is resident at LabCentral in Cambridge, and recently closed a $3 million Series A round. Angiex founders discovered VEGF-A, have been recognized as the world's leading experts in tumor blood vessel biology, developed new methods for per cell mRNA quantification, founded four companies, and wrote a best-selling diet book. *Source:* https://angiex.com/
Kymera Therapeutics	Kymera Therapeutics is a seed-stage therapeutics company focused on targeting the traditionally undruggable proteome within key pathways involved in inflammation, immunity, and oncology. Its approach combines the power of effective genetic silencing with the flexibility and drug-like properties of small molecules to harness the body's innate protein regulation machinery. *Source:* https://labcentral.org/resident-companies/kymera/
ReviveMed	ReviveMed is a precision-medicine platform that leverages the data from small molecules or metabolites. Metabolomics (which is the study of small molecules such as glucose or cholesterol) is essential for developing the right therapeutics for the right patients. However, because identifying a large set of metabolites for each patient is costly and slow, metabolomic data has been under-utilized – and the firm aim at filling this gap. ReviveMed technology, which was developed at MIT and published in Nature Methods, uniquely overcomes the difficulty of using a large set of metabolomic data, and transform these data into actionable insight. Currently, they are working with a few strategic partners from leading pharma/biotech companies, while developing their own metabolomics based therapeutics. *Source:* www.revive-med.com

Source: Author's own elaboration

Table 3.6 Expert interviews: list of participants

Position	*Organization*	*Stakeholder*
Full Professor	MIT Department of Chemical Engineering	University and research institutes
General Counsel and Vice President for Academic and Workforce Program	Massachusetts Life Science Center	Government
Chief Executive Officer	Obsidian	Entrepreneurship–biotech
Chief Executive Officer	Angiex	Entrepreneurship–start-up
Chief Executive Officer	Kymera Therapeutics	Entrepreneurship–start-up
Chief Executive Officer	ReviveMed	Entrepreneurship–spin-off
Alliance Manager	Alnylam	Entrepreneurship–start-up
Research Associate	Novartis	Corporate
Senior Vice President, R&D Strategy and External Innovation	Ironwood Pharmaceuticals, Inc.	Corporate

Source: Author's own elaboration

Insights on the LIS successful network composition have been gained by exploring:

- Which relationships have a greater impact on knowledge transfer;
- For which relationships being in spatial proximity with the partners was more valuable.

The experts were asked to discuss those types of relationships that were more frequently implemented in their practices of innovation processes and provide insights on those that best contribute to knowledge transfer and about the importance of being in spatial proximity with the partners for each specific type of relationship.

3.5 Conclusions

This chapter has illustrated the methodological approach and the research design selected for the exploration of the relational dimension of LIS. The insights on the biopharma industry main features in both terms of R&D dynamics and forms of inter-organizational cooperation served to prove the suitability of the industry for the empirical purposes of this study. Indeed, the high level of specialization of the activities and the high risks and costs associated to the drug development process make cooperation particularly crucial to actors' competitiveness. The description of the Greater Boston biopharma innovation system, through the provision of its historical background and metrics of performance, served to depict this system as a benchmark of success in the field whose implication in terms of network structure and portfolio are of particular importance for emerging systems. Finally, the discussion about the two selected research techniques and the emphasis on their points of strength and weaknesses allowed us to appreciate the advantages deriving from a combined approach to broaden the reach of the analytic framework. The next chapter will discuss main findings derived from data analysis and provide a theoretical framework for the study of LIS relational perspective.

References

Audretsch, D. B., & Stephan, P. E. (1996). Company-scientist locational links: The case of biotechnology. *The American Economic Review, 86*(3), 641–652.

Basole, R. C., Clear, T., Hu, M., Mehrotra, H., & Stasko, J. (2013). Understanding interfirm relationships in business ecosystems with interactive visualization. *IEEE Transactions on Visualization and Computer Graphics, 19*(12), 2526–2535.

Baxter, P., & Jack, S. (2008). Qualitative case study methodology: Study design and implementation for novice researchers. *The Qualitative Report, 13*(4), 544–559.

Bianchi, M., Cavaliere, A., Chiaroni, D., Frattini, F., & Chiesa, V. (2011). Organisational modes for Open Innovation in the bio-pharmaceutical industry: An exploratory analysis. *Technovation, 31*(1), 22–33.

Bogner, A., & Menz, W. (2002). Das theoriegenerierende Experteninterview. In *Das Experteninterview* (pp. 33–70). VS Verlag für Sozialwissenschaften.

Breznitz, S. M. (2015). Invention & reinvention: The evolution of San Diego's innovation economy by Mary Lindenstein Walshok and Abraham J. Shragge, Stanford, CA: Stanford University Press, 2014. *Economic Geography, 91*(1), 117–118.

Burt, R. S. (1992). *Structural holes: The structure of social capital competition.* Cambridge, MA: Harvard University Press.

Capellari, S., Chies, L., De Stefano, D., & Puggioni, A. (2016). *L'analisi di rete per capire il mercato del lavoro. I flussi di assunzione di laureati e dottori di ricerca nel Friuli Venezia Giulia nel periodo 2005–2014.* EUT Edizioni Università di Trieste.

Capello, R., & Faggian, A. (2005). Collective learning and relational capital in local innovation processes. *Regional Studies, 39*(1), 75–87.

Corbin, J., & Morse, J. M. (2003). The unstructured interactive interview: Issues of reciprocity and risks when dealing with sensitive topics. *Qualitative Inquiry, 9*, 335–354.

Corbin, J., & Strauss, A. (2008). *Basics of qualitative research: Techniques and procedures for developing grounded theory* (3rd ed.). Thousand Oaks, CA: Sage Publications.

Davis, D., Davis, M. E., Jadad, A., Perrier, L., Rath, D., Ryan, D., . . . Zwarenstein, M. (2003). The case for knowledge translation: Shortening the journey from evidence to effect. *BMJ, 327*(7405), 33–35.

Davis, G. F., Yoo, M., & Baker, W. E. (2003). The small world of the American corporate elite, 1982-2001. *Strategic Organization, 1*(3), 301–326.

De Bruijn-Geraets, D. P., Van Eijk-Hustings, Y. J., & Vrijhoef, H. J. (2014). Evaluating newly acquired authority of nurse practitioners and physician assistants for reserved medical procedures in the Netherlands: A study protocol. *Journal of Advanced Nursing, 70*(11), 2673–2682.

Ensing, E. (2017). Biopharma R&D partnerships: From David & Goliath to Networked R&D (by Thong, R. (2016). Phizz Rx Publishing: London, pp. 272). *R&D Management, 47*(2), 330–331.

Ferretti, M., & Parmentola, A. (2015). Local innovation systems in emerging countries. In *The creation of local innovation systems in emerging countries* (pp. 7–36). Cham, Switzerland: Springer International Publishing.

Freeman, C. (2002). Continental, national and sub-national innovation systems: Complementarity and economic growth. *Research Policy, 31*(2), 191–211.

Gambardella, A. (1995). *Science and innovation: The US pharmaceutical industry during the 1980s.* Cambridge: Cambridge University Press.

Gray, D. E. (2009). *Doing research in the real world* (2nd ed.). Thousand Oaks, CA: Sage Publications.

Halinen, A. (2012). *Relationship marketing in professional services: A study of agency-client dynamics in the advertising sector.* London: Routledge.

Hartley, R. F. (1994). *Management mistakes & successes.* New York: John Wiley & Sons.

JJL U.S. Life Science 2016. Retrieved from https://www.us.jll.com/en/trends-and-insights/research/life-sciences-industry-trends

Johansson, P. (2003). Madfilm: A multimodal approach to handle search and organization in a movie recommendation system. In *Proceedings of the 1st Nordic Symposium on Multimodal Communication* (pp. 53–65). CST, Center for Sprogteknologi.

Kajikawa, Y., Takeda, Y., Sakata, I., & Matsushima, K. (2010). Multiscale analysis of interfirm networks in regional clusters. *Technovation, 30*(3), 168–180.

Kohlbacher, F. (2006). The use of qualitative content analysis in case study research. In *Forum Qualitative Sozialforschung/Forum: Qualitative Social Research* (Vol. 7, No. 1, pp. 1–30). Institut für Qualitative Forschung.

Kohn, A. (1997). How not to teach values: A critical look at character education. *Phi Delta Kappan, 78*(6), 429–439.

Meuser, M., & Nagel, U. (1991). ExpertInneninterviews – vielfach erprobt, wenig bedacht. In *Qualitativ-empirische sozialforschung* (pp. 441–471). VS Verlag für Sozialwissenschaften.

Milne, C. P., & Malins, A. (2012). *Academic–industry partnerships for biopharmaceutical research & development: Advancing medical science in the US.* Tuft Center for the Study of Drug Development.

Mizruchi, M. S. (1992). *The structure of corporate political action: Interfirm relations and their consequences.* Cambridge, MA: Harvard University Press.

Moody, J., & White, D. R. (2003). Structural cohesion and embeddedness: A hierarchical concept of social groups. *American Sociological Review*, 68(1), 103–127.

Owen-Smith, J., & Powell, W. W. (2004). Knowledge networks as channels and conduits: The effects of spillovers in the Boston biotechnology community. *Organization Science, 15*(1), 5–21.

Powell, W. W., Koput, K. W., & Doerr, L. S. (1996). Interorganizational Collaboration and the Locus of Innovation: Networks of Learning in Biotechnology. *Administrative Science Quarterly*, 41(1), 116–145.

Preqin Ltd. (2017). Retreived from https://www.preqin.com/

Reynolds, E. B., & Uygun, Y. (2017). Strengthening advanced manufacturing innovation ecosystems: The case of Massachusetts. *Technological Forecasting and Social Change, 136*, 178–191.

Reynolds, E. B., Zylberberg, E., & Del Campo, M. V. (2016). *Brazil's role in the biopharmaceutical global value chain.* Working Papers. MIT-IPC. Retrieved from https://ipc. mit.edu/sites/default/files/documents/16-004. pdf.

Russell, M. G., Huhtamäki, J., Still, K., Rubens, N., & Basole, R. C. (2015). Relational capital for shared vision in innovation ecosystems. *Triple Helix, 2*(1), 1–36.

Russell, M. G., Still, K., Huhtamäki, J., Yu, C., & Rubens, N. (2011). Transforming innovation ecosystems through shared vision and network orchestration. In *Triple Helix IX International Conference*, Stanford, CA, USA.

Saxenian, A. (1996). *Regional advantage*. Cambridge, MA: Harvard University Press.
Simoni, M., & Schiavone, F. (2009). *Il ruolo della grande impresa nello sviluppo dei poli innovativi*. McGraw-Hill.
Soy, S. K. (1997). *The case study as a research method*. Unpublished Paper, University of Texas at Austin.
Still, K., Huhtamäki, J., Russell, M. G., & Rubens, N. (2014). Insights for orchestrating innovation ecosystems: The case of EIT ICT Labs and data-driven network visualisations. *International Journal of Technology Management*, *66*(2–3), 243–265.
Streb, C. K. (2010). Exploratory case study. *Encyclopedia of Case Study Research*, *1*, 373–375.
Teece, D. J. (1986). Profiting from technological innovation: Implications for integration, collaboration, licensing and public policy. *Research Policy*, *15*(6), 285–305.
Ter Wal, A. L. J. (2014). The dynamics of the inventor network in German biotechnology: Geographic proximity versus triadic closure. *Journal of Economic Geography*, *14*(3), 589–620.
U.S. Census Bureau, 2015. Retreived from https://www.census.gov/
Wasserman, S., & Faust, K. (1994). *Social network analysis: Methods and applications* (Vol. 8). Cambridge: Cambridge University Press.
Welser, H. T., Gleave, E., Fisher, D., & Smith, M. (2007). Visualizing the signatures of social roles in online discussion groups. *Journal of Social Structure*, *8*(2), 1–32.
Yin, R. K. (1994). Discovering the future of the case study. Method in evaluation research. *Evaluation Practice*, *15*(3), 283–290.
Yin, R. K. (2009). *Case study research: Design and methods*. Applied Social Research Methods Series, 219. London: Sage.
Yin, R. K. (2015). *Qualitative research from start to finish*. New York: Guilford Press.

4 Results from the empirical study

4.1 Network structural configuration in a successful LIS

4.1.1 Results from the social network analysis

The network resulting from the sample of organizations consists of 281 connected nodes and 381 edges, with a diameter of 13. From the analysis of network composition, it emerges that venture deals represent the most frequent type of tie in our sample (58.1%), followed by IP transfer (20.8%). R&D partnerships and other biotech deals account for 9% each, and finally, joint ventures and academic spin-offs/corporate spinouts represent only 2.2% and 0.9% of the network portfolio, respectively (Figure 4.1). Tables 4.1 and 4.2 report findings from the social network analysis conducted on relational data available for the Greater Boston biopharma system and network metrics have been interpreted as indicators of LIS relational capital.

At the micro-level, the computation of *betweenness centrality* served to identify the top 20 actors in terms of centrality position in the network. Indeed, *high betweenness centrality* values indicate that a node has a connecting role between the different parts of the overall network and contributes to identify key stakeholders within innovation systems.

Top positions are occupied mainly by large venture capital firms (e.g. New Enterprise Associates, Third Rock Ventures, Polaris Partners) and pharmaceutical companies with a venture arms (CRISPR; Pfizer, Inc.; Celgene; Novartis Venture Funds; AstraZeneca Pharmaceutical, LP) (Table 4.1).

At the structural level, metrics of density, average degree, modularity and small worlds properties have been computed to gain insights about the overall configuration of the network (Table 4.2). More specifically, the *ratio of edge to node* has been calculated to show the number of connections between nodes in the system, which indicates a high level of engagement of the network and density, which in turn, expresses the number of actual linkages divided by the maximum number of possible linkages, has been calculated to provide indication of network *vitality* (Russell, Huhtamäki, Still, Rubens, & Basole, 2015). Values of density close to 0 indicate that the network is *poorly connected*, and conversely, when these are close to 1, they exemplify a high level of connectivity in the

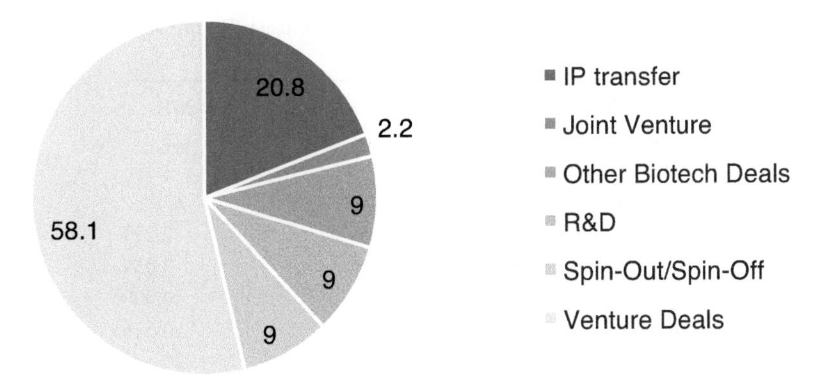

Figure 4.1 Network portfolio composition: Greater Boston Area (2012–2017)

Source: Author's own elaboration from Preqin Ltd. (2017) and *Pharma & MedTech Business Intelligence* (2017)

Table 4.1 Top 20 actors: betweenness centrality in the Greater Boston Area (2012–2017)

Rank	*Organization*	*Value*
1	Rhythm Pharmaceuticals, Inc.	0.225
2	New Enterprise Associates	0.176
3	Third Rock Ventures	0.155
4	CRISPR	0.154
5	Polaris Partners	0.107
6	Pfizer, Inc.	0.105
7	SR One (GSK)	0.103
8	Ra Pharma	0.102
9	Celgene	0.094
10	MPM Capital	0.087
11	Kala Pharmaceuticals, Inc.	0.084
12	Moderna	0.084
13	Novartis Venture Funds	0.081
14	Navitor	0.081
15	Aileron Therapeutics, Inc.	0.077
16	Lightstones Ventures	0.076
17	Atlas Venture	0.071
18	Syros Pharmaceuticals, Inc.	0.069
19	Ctabasis Pharmaceuticals	0.066
20	AstraZeneca Pharmaceuticals	0.065

Source: Author's own elaboration

Table 4.2 Social network analysis metrics: Greater Boston Area (2012–2017)

# of nodes	281
# of edges	323
Ratio of edge to node	1.15
Network diameter	13
Average degree	2.299
Average weighted degree	3.039
Graph density	0.008
Modularity	0.626
Connected components	120
Average clustering coefficient	0.059
Average path length	4.458

Source: Author's own elaboration

network. In the case of the GBA biopharma LIS, the graph shows a relatively low value of density (0.008), suggesting that the network is relatively sparse (Balland, De Vaan, & Boschma, 2012) and characterized by the presence of structural holes (Ahuja, 2000).

The average degree, that is, the average number of available connections per entity, reveals insights about the relational potential and expresses, on average, the number of organizations' partners. In the case of the GBA biopharma LIS, the *average degree* and the *average weighted degree* (interactions weighted according to their frequency) show values that indicate an average level of engagement of the network's actors with partners in spatial propinquity (Kajikawa, Takeda, Sakata, & Matsushima, 2010; Still, Huhtamäki, Russell, & Rubens, 2014; Salavisa, Sousa, & Fontes, 2012). At the meso-structural level, *modularity* scores (0.626) and the high number of *connected components* (120) suggest a high tendency of network's actors to form sub-groups where interactions occur more easily. In fact, a connected component of an undirected graph is a maximal set of nodes, in a way that a path connects each pair of nodes. Connected components constitute a partition of the set of graph nodes, which means that connected components are non-empty, but rather pairwise disjoints. Additionally, the network has been analyzed from a *small world* perspective, by calculating the *average path length* and the *average clustering coefficient* (Watts & Strogatz, 1998). Following Kajikawa et al. (2010), the *average path length* (i.e. the average graph distance between all pairs of nodes) is fundamental for the assessment of the network performance as it indicates that a node can have an easier and quicker access to other actors with less effort, thus accessing to a larger amount of knowledge or information. Generally speaking, a small value of average path length indicates a small diameter of the network, which in turns suggests that organizations in the network can pool resources through a smaller number of paths and structural holes are buried. On the other hand, the *clustering coefficient* represents the extent to which nodes connected to *i* are also linked to each other, and the *average cluster coefficient* shows the system's overall connectivity based on local relationships, suggesting a greater accumulation of social capital.

It is argued that small world configuration allows achieving both advantages of closed and open networks. In fact, while a network with a small path length sustains network closure (as it allows information to circulate more easily and quickly through a less number of paths and structural holes), a network with high clustering coefficient suggests that larger social capital is accumulated, which is a benefit typical of open and sparser networks.

The GBA innovation system presents relatively high values for both the first small world property (i.e. *average path length* [4.458]) and the second one (i.e. *clustering coefficient score*; Kajikawa et al., 2010 [0.058]), thus confirming its structural tendency toward a more open configuration, with specific implications in terms of a more diversified relational capital through less redundant and weaker ties. Visualizations of the GBA network are provided in Figure 4.2. While the former highlights the tendency of forming dyadic and triplets forms of interactions as

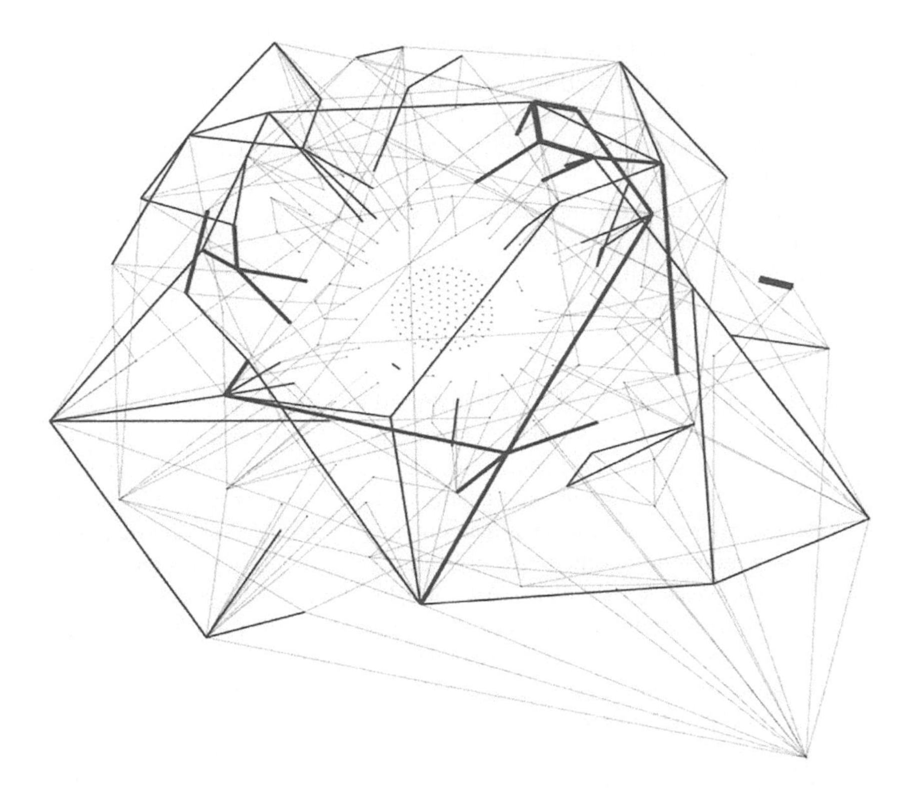

Figure 4.2 Greater Boston biopharma innovation system: network structure (2012–2017)

Source: Author's own elaboration through Gephi

well as visual information about their frequency, the latter presents the distribution of the different types of relationships composing the relational dataset.

In conclusion, the GBA biopharma LIS appears to be characterized by an open structure with structural holes and the tendency of vertices to form small groups where interactions are more frequent. Finally, bridging functions appear to be mostly undertaken by large venture capital firms and pharmaceutical companies with venture arms.

However, due to the lack of exact benchmark parameters for network structural metrics in the network literature, these results should be taken as a reference for future comparative analysis.

4.2 Network composition in a successful LIS

4.2.1 The most common practices of innovation-driven interactions within the LIS

From the results of expert interviews, it emerged that the most frequent practices of innovation-driven interactions with the actors in the area are:

1. Value added supply agreements;
2. Venture capital and seed investments;
3. Agreements for the access and use of infrastructure;
4. Co-participation in thematic associations and symposia;
5. Board interlocks;
6. Formal and informal industry-university agreements for the mobility of human resources;
7. Sponsored research;
8. Intellectual property transfer;
9. R&D strategic alliances.

In general terms, it emerged that partnerships that promote connectivity among different disciplines are more likely to bring potential for innovation and that these should be incentivized through, for example, thematic initiatives (e.g. student clubs), which are able to pool talents with a diverse set of capabilities and knowledge. There is a common agreement among the interviewees that cross-disciplinary interaction contributes to bring complementary skills and smooth the so-called *knowledge disabilities*. Additionally, there is a large consensus that informal relations, compared to more structured and institutionalized alliances, represent an easier way of *know-how trading* (cit. "the more formal the relationship the lower opportunity for transfer of information") due to the potential of learning through face-to face conversation, facilitated by embeddedness (Former Dean of MIT Department of Chemical Engineering). The physical proximity of different ecosystem's actors turns out to be very important as it stimulates mechanisms of trust through the building of social relations (cit. "relationships are important because relationships between people are important") and that the emergence of a "culture of trust" is vital for the ecosystem performance (Former Dean of MIT Department of Chemical Engineering).

4.2.2 *Types of relationships that contribute to knowledge transfer*

More specifically, it emerged that knowledge transfer is particularly enhanced in:

1 Co-participation in thematic associations and symposia;
2 Agreements for the access and use of infrastructure;
3 Venture capital and seed investments;
4 Formal and informal industry-university agreements for the mobility of human resources.

With regards to *co-participation in thematic associations and symposia*, as in the case of the Neuroscience Consortium, which was created by Mass Life Science with the aim of filling the gaps in research funds through the organization of periodical operative meetings between different stakeholders in the field of neurodegenerative diseases, it emerged that this practice was particularly important for knowledge transfer as it allows the sharing of experiences in the pre-commercial phase (i.e. target identification and validation). One of the main issues is that failures in the industry are not generally made public and therefore bringing different stakeholders around the table allows avoiding the duplication of efforts including mistakes, thus avoiding redundancy of information and enhancing innovation potential. Other indirect benefits to knowledge transfer deriving from this type of practice, regard primarily the achievement of time and cost efficiencies in relationship-seeking activities (as the consortium gathers all major academic centers in the area) and the alignment of visions and missions of the different epistemic communities by promoting dialogue among them and leading to a collective resolution of problems. Similarly, but to a much lower extent of formalization, the Alliance Manager from Ironwood reported his experience in arranging periodical target specific symposia for sharing pre-competitive knowledge with competitors and major research actors in the area (e.g. Novartis, MIT, Harvard and Tufts) for the development of a specific molecule. These meetings, which have a grassroots origin (from company scientists' initiative), take place in an informal way – "It's a mix of social and science" (cit. Ironwood's CEO) – mostly during a poster session, with five to seven participants and a couple of speakers. One interesting point is that, despite the high confidentiality of the information exchanged, there is no need of non-disclosure formal agreements due to the reported high level of trust and mutual understanding that naturally emerges among the participants.

Second, *venture capital and seed investments* relationships turn out to be ground for the transfer of new knowledge due to the complementarity of the skills between innovative firms' scientific know-how and investors' support for business operations. As reported by Kymera's CEO, especially in the case of funding venture capital (VC), the start-up is usually provided with support regarding every aspect of the business management, including assistance for hiring the right people and for seeking potential partnerships to exploit the developed innovation at its best.

As for the *agreements for the access and use of infrastructure*, their efficacy in terms of knowledge transfer result from a spillover effect of the environment provided by hosting organizations. From the experience of Obsidian, apart from the well-known advantages in terms of visibility and costs efficiencies deriving from renting a space within an innovation center, it is also the opportunity of *casual encounters* with industry operators that enhances the chance of knowledge exchange in this case. Also, incubators and accelerators generally offer services of business consultancy to scientists and engineers that lack capabilities in this field.

Finally, *industry-university agreements for the mobility of human resources* are deemed by the experts to be one of the most fruitful relationships in terms of knowledge transfer. The Massachusetts Life Science Internship Challenge and the Northeastern Co-Op (Cooperative Education and Career Development) are some of the examples appointed as best practices in promoting knowledge transfer between industry and academia. The former provides a platform to facilitate the placement of college students in life science by subsidizing paid internships hosted by companies in the area, while the latter constitutes a powerful learning model that promotes intellectual and professional growth by integrating classroom learning with practical experience. In so doing, on the one hand real-world experience enhances the potential for innovation of academic human capital and on the other, the partners pursue a cost-effective strategy for hiring and training a talented workforce.

With regards to *board interlocks, sponsored research* and *IP transfer*, the process of knowledge transfer is less accentuated. More specifically, interlocking directorates are considered to be more useful for establishing new partnerships as a direct consequence of the exploitation of board members' diverse networks. Most interviewees agreed on the fact that knowledge transfer efficacy really depends on the board composition. As a way of illustration, Ironwood's CEO reported the advantages of having the CEO of Blue Cross and Blue Shield of Massachusetts, Inc. on their board of directors as he gave them "the perspective of what it means to deliver products to patients to deliver healthcare". Also, the interviewees reported that knowledge transfer manifests more explicitly through the establishment of ad hoc scientific advisory committees where the composition of members (often from academia) is more flexible, according to the innovation's specific issues under discussion.

Sponsored research and more in general relationships with academia contribute to knowledge transfer depending on the stage of the innovation process. Industry experts agreed on the fact that, in general terms, academic investigators are really good at idea generation – "to think outside the box" – while they tend to lack competencies concerning the product development cycle. Partnering with academic centers of excellence may give access to the newest thinking and potential disruptive ideas as well as very specific expertise. In the second case, sponsored research may take the form of a *fee-for-service*, as in the case in which the company is willing to use a specific model to understand how their compound behaves with a specific disease.

IP transfer is traditionally renowned as a practice of knowledge transfer despite many of the experts reported that the tendency toward a more *hands-off approach* limits the amount of information exchanged to the operative phases and not to the innovation process itself. As claimed by the CEO of Angiex, while discussing his experience with the Beth Israel Deaconess Medical Center where the company in-licensed some IP: "It is very difficult to transfer knowledge and the IP transfer process is different from knowledge transfer process. IP transfer process is essentially work for lawyers and technology venture offices that are trying to find a home for patents and that do not necessarily know that much about the science behind things". The IP is generally developed by academics, therefore, in typical companies where the academics who developed the IP did not leave the hospital, they typically became advisors to the company (sitting on the advisory board) and received stocks in exchange for taking care of that knowledge transfer. In these cases, the IP developers are able to give company's employees some background about the technology and the work that was done in their academic institution.

4.2.3 The role of spatial proximity for the different types of relationships

While asking for which specific types of relationship being in spatial proximity with the partners was more valuable, the experts refer to:

- Agreements for the access and use of infrastructure;
- VC and seed investments;
- Co-participation in thematic associations;
- Strategic alliance.

More precisely, proximity is at the core of the *innovation centers* concept and some of the experts that we interviewed have operations in different of these innovation centers, as in the case of Obsidian, which used to have operations distributed in three different facilities in Cambridge (LabCentral, Cambridge Biolabs and Broad Institute). Therefore, it is clear that in case of *agreements for the access and use of infrastructure*, operating in the same area of the hosting structure is fundamental. According to the experts, embeddedness itself is favored by the presence of incubators and co-working spaces that multiply the networking opportunities thanks to their strategic design that promotes *casual encounters*, as in the case of the Koch Center, where engineers and scientists are located on the same floor.

As for *venture capital and seed investments*, the importance of spatial proximity is mainly explained by the frequency of interactions required – especially at the seed stage – and the need of establishing trust mechanisms with the partners. As affirmed by Kymera's CEO, "personal ties play a key role in fostering relationships with investors and living in the same place makes a difference". Proximity allows to have more frequent interactions with a network of operators in the area that may eventually function as a *talent validation* device, which turns out to be particularly useful for risky operations as in the case of VC and seed funds. While exploring the relationship between Kymera and Atlas Venture – a VC company headquartered in Kendall Square (Cambridge) – it emerged that it is not uncommon for VC companies to host their portfolio companies in their office spaces. Also, especially in the case of VC founders, relationships tend to be long-term, thus implying an investment not only in money but also in time, which – as reported by Alnylam's CEO – allows for a more efficient corporate resource management.

Proximity is particularly important also in the case of *co-participation in thematic associations*, as it enables to enhance interactions outside the association's meetings and to build trust mechanisms, which are particularly important if we consider that many of the members are competitors and their frequent interactions contribute to align their vision, as reported by MLSC.

Finally, while exploring the 10-year *strategic alliance* between Novartis and the MIT Department of Chemical Engineering, the former dean highlighted how R&D partnerships between industry and university have evolved over time from covering a less significant share of funds and following a more hands-off approach to becoming more strategic. In his view, nowadays companies have a clear understanding of their long-term goals and present a higher level of engagement in university activities, which in turn requires more frequent interaction between them and the academic department. Also, in the case of *strategic alliances*, geographic proximity would decrease the so-called *collaboration risk* (e.g. project orphaning; divergence of missions and goals).

Conversely, spatial proximity with partners within *value added supply relationships*, especially with CROs, does not seem to play a key role. As frequently reported by interviewees, "CROs can be anywhere", and this is partly explained by the high degree of standardization of many of the outsourced services in the drug development industry and the stage of the life science R&D cycle when these interactions happen (i.e. *target validation*). Only in those cases where contract manufacturing requires a high degree of customization, geographic proximity may play a more significant role.

4.3 An analytical framework for the study of LIS performance from a relational perspective

From the results of the analyses reported in Sections 4.1 and 4.2, it emerges that the GBA biopharma LIS is an open network with structural holes where bridging functions are mostly undertaken by large venture capital firms and pharmaceutical companies with a venture arm, and where vertices tend to form small groups in which the mutual interactions are more frequent. Also, the relationships that enhance knowledge transfer and for which spatial proximity is more important are traceable to those that foster cross-disciplinary interaction and match complementary resources (financial and technical) and skills (business support and scientific capabilities), that is, *co-participation in thematic associations and symposia*, *agreements for the access and use of infrastructure* and *venture capital and seed investments* (Figure 4.3). It is worth mentioning how the closed network structure was appointed by Saxenian (1996) as one of the determining causes of decline in the Boston innovation system on semiconductor industry – known as Route 128 – in favor of the more open and horizontal network of Silicon

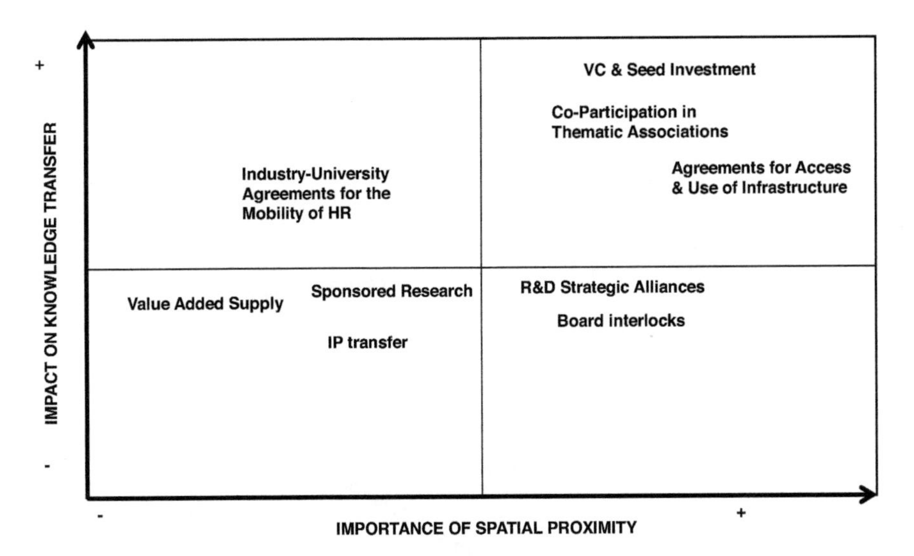

Figure 4.3 Network portfolio in the biopharma LIS in the Greater Boston Area

Source: Author's own elaboration

Valley. Results from SNA are coherent with the outcome of expert interviews that suggest that an open network with non-redundant ties is preferable in terms of positive impact on innovation systems' performance.

More specifically, the co-participation in thematic associations and symposia contributes to the level of efficiency of the innovation system as a whole, as it improves information exchange between actors in the same field with implications in terms of avoiding the replication of failures in the pre-commercial phase and in terms of aligning vision and missions, thus leading to a collective resolution of R&D problems, as well as for cutting the costs and times of partnerships' seeking and identifying the gaps in research areas. The agreements for the access and use of infrastructure, which are reflected in the proliferation of innovation centers in the area (co-working spaces, accelerators and incubators), positively affect the innovation system performance by exerting a knowledge spillover effect within the environment these provide to their residents, by enhancing those casual encounters and visibility to target-oriented partners and providing resources in terms of both business support and facilities. As a consequence, the initial costs for developing an innovation are reduced and the market barriers for start-ups with a limited experience in business know-how can be smoothened by those benefits deriving from the knowledge production output for the whole system. Similarly, VC and seed investments represent an important vehicle for the transfer of complementary assets and represent a key player for the development of innovative products along the whole innovation process. In general terms, it is possible to argue that the innovation system performance is enhanced by those types of partnerships that promote connectivity among different disciplines and

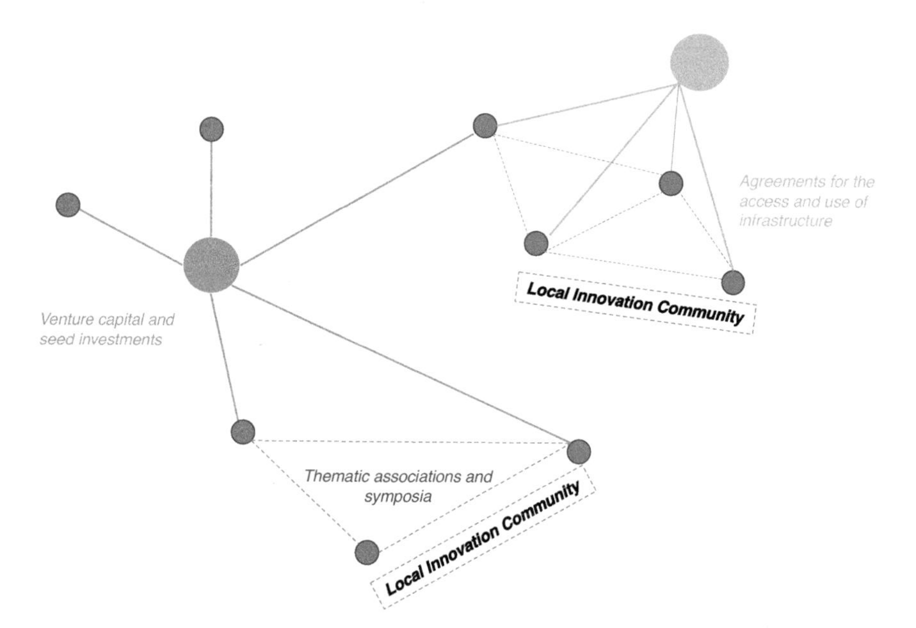

Figure 4.4 Local innovation communities and their role in open networks

Source: Author's own elaboration

sectors as these contribute to smooth *knowledge disabilities* and *know-how trading*. This network portfolio is coherent also with the tendency, at the structural level, of being divided in small groups where interactions occur more easily, as in the case of specific thematic associations (e.g. the Neuroscience Consortium or the Massachusetts Biotechnology Council) or sector-specific innovation centers (e.g. LabCentral), so as to form local innovation communities that focus their joint effort on specific R&D targets within the LIS. These local innovation communities are therefore characterized by a high-intensity knowledge transfer through organizations of different nature and a high frequency of interactions, yet with a low degree of formalization, co-localized in the same geographical area (Figure 4.4).

4.3.1 *Main implications of the study*

The goal of this work is to explore the relational dimension of LIS by deriving evidence from the study of a successful case and derive propositions to be tested in future studies. More specifically, two research questions have been formulated for this purpose:

> (RQ1) Which is the configuration of the network structure in a successful local innovation system?
> (RQ2) Which portfolio of relationships is implemented in a successful local innovation system?

These research questions have been formulated in order to capture both aspects of LIS's relational dimension (network structure and network portfolio composition). From the results of the study conducted on the GBA biopharma LIS it is possible to derive a set of propositions, which are intended to be tested in future studies and to develop practical implications for those regions whose innovation system is at its early stage of development. More specifically, with regards to the network structure, it emerged that:

P1. *LIS performance is impacted by its network structure.*

Indeed, the positional and structural indicators computed through the social network analysis suggest that the performance of LIS is positively impacted by a sparse network where bridging roles are mostly undertaken by venture capital firms or large biopharmaceutical companies with a venture arm. Therefore, a sub-proposition may be derived:

P1.1 *A highly performant LIS is characterized by an open network structure with structural holes.* Also, indicators at the meso-structural level suggest that the performance of LIS is positively impacted by the level of network's division into modules (i.e. groups, clusters or communities) in which nodes have dense connections with those belonging to the same module, but weak connections with nodes in different modules. Therefore,

P1.2 *A highly performant LIS is characterized by a high level of division of a network into modules.* As a second step, network portfolio composition has been analyzed according two dimensions namely, the *impact for knowledge transfer*, considered as a precondition of innovation creation, and the *importance of spatial proximity* which, in turn, is a precondition for the frequency of the interactions and for the emergence of trust mechanisms (Granovetter, 1985). Weak ties result from the embeddedness of actors within a certain spatial configuration. Figure 4.3 shows the relationships with high scores for both dimensions (VC and seed investments, co-participation in thematic associations and symposia and agreements for the access and use of infrastructure). With reference to *VC and seed investment*, despite the formalization that characterize this form of tie, it emerged that it is mainly the exchange of complementary skills (business support and scientific capabilities) and the advantages in terms of reputation for the start-ups within VC portfolio that play a major role. The relationships that are established between VC companies and start-ups allow the latter to access to VC's network with large pharmaceutical companies and give them credibility and talent validation for further partnerships and future growth. The way through which these relationships emerge and grow is considered to be highly enhanced by the spatial proximity that multiply the chances of casual encounters and visibility for those start-ups willing to receive funds. Additionally, the spatial propinquity allows VC to achieve a more effective monitoring and continuous support to their start-up partners. With regards to *co-participation in thematic associations and symposia*, spatial proximity of the partners ensures the frequency of the interaction between members, who can establish relationships outside the periodical meetings and form further partnerships based on trust mechanisms resulting from the common affiliation and mission toward specific target research areas. Also, these relationships promote the convening of actors of different nature and disciplines, which ensures the non-redundancy of the exchanged information and the transfer of different (and complementary) practices to tackle with specific research challenges. Finally, the agreements for the access and use of infrastructure are deemed to provide knowledge spillovers for the actors who physically locate in innovation centers and foster an environment of informal cooperation deriving from their daily interaction, which contribute to the emergence of mechanisms of trust that are key for potential cooperation in specific target areas on the basis of weak ties.

Therefore, from what was observed it is possible to suggest that:

P2. *LIS performance is impacted by its network portfolio composition.*

More specifically, the form of the observed types of relationships, with specific reference to the way through which transfer of information occurs and future partnerships arise, appears to be mainly based on trust and reputational effects without the necessity of contractual bounds (informal ties) whose existence is stimulated by spatial proximity. This, in turn, suggests that the composition of a network portfolio is predominated by the presence of weak ties. Therefore:

P2.1 *A highly performant LIS is characterized by a network portfolio dominated by weak ties.* Additionally, the content of the observed types of relationships, with specific reference to the diversity of the nature of engaged partners and the complementarity of the resource exchanged, suggests that:

P2.2 *A highly performant LIS is characterized by a network portfolio dominated by non-redundant ties.*

Finally, by combining the results deriving from both the analysis of the structure and the portfolio of the network, it is possible to observe the tendency of actors from different epistemic communities to convene in small groups around specific thematic areas where knowledge transfer occurs through loose ties whose frequency is ensured by their spatial proximity, that are able to span the structural holes typical of the open structure of the network (i.e. local innovation communities). Therefore,

P3. *A highly performant LIS is characterized by the presence of local innovation communities.* Conclusively, this work suggests that the performance of an LIS is positively affected by the openness of its network structure, the weakness of the relationships between its actors and the tendency of the actors to form local innovation communities (Figure 4.5).

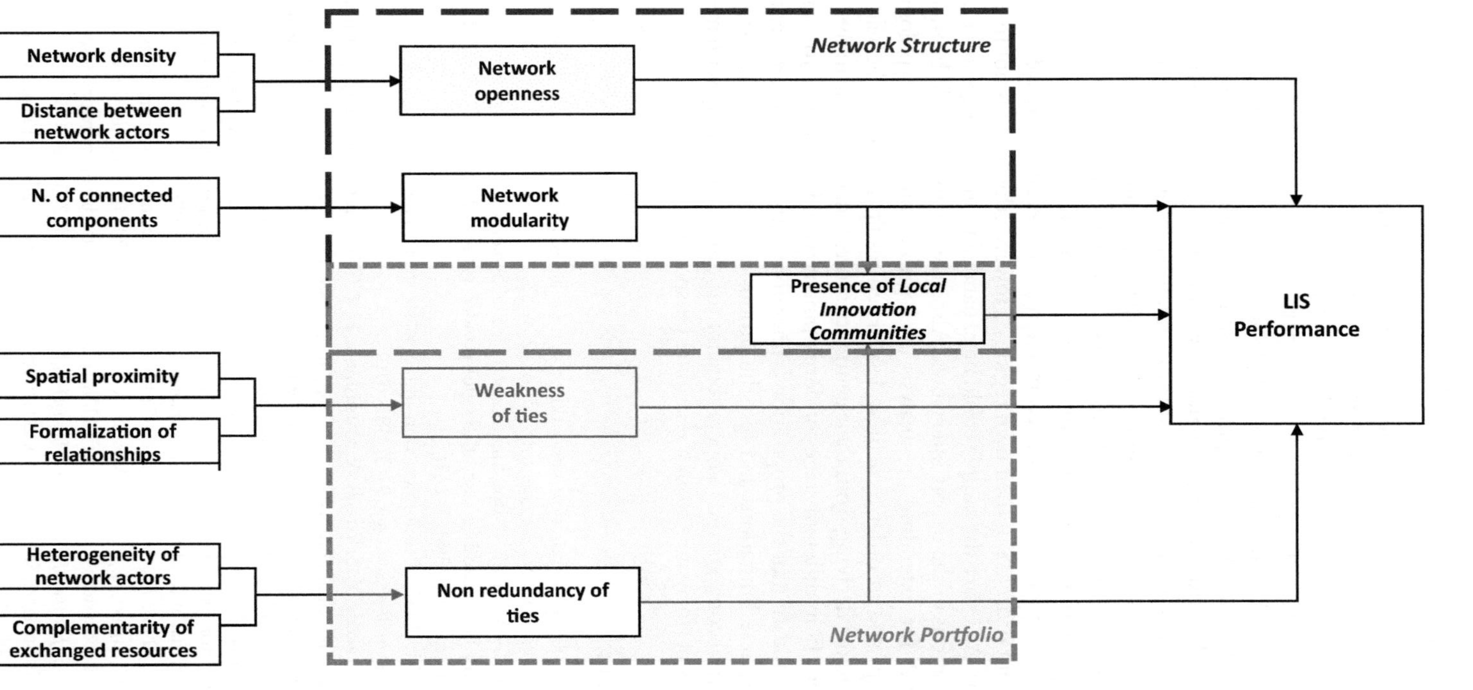

Figure 4.5 Analytical framework for the study of LIS performance from a relational perspective

Source: Author's own elaboration

4.4 Conclusions

This study contributes to the debate about the optimal configuration of network structure (e.g. closure network vs. structural holes), suggesting that an open structure is preferable for determining the successful performance of an LIS. Additionally, from a methodological perspective, it contributes to meet the challenges related to the adoption of a holistic approach by capturing the heterogeneous nature of LIS demography, whereas most studies limit their analyses to inter-firm relationships and at the node level. Finally, the study provides insights into the network portfolio composition, which has been underexplored in LIS literature, allowing for the identification of those relationships considered more fruitful for fostering the innovation processes from a local perspective.

In particular, this last aspect of the study's contribution has practical implications for policy makers and those actors willing to undertake an active role in the development of an LIS in their own regions. However, this study is not free from limitations. As a start, the sample could be expanded to include a greater number of organizations in the expert interviews. Also, new databases could be included in the SNA for extending the analysis on a greater number of typologies of partnerships and in order to achieve less biased results regarding the nature of bridging actors deriving from their centrality score. Finally, a comparative study with other LIS in different stages of development would contribute to a greater extent of validation of the propositions. Therefore, future scholars are invited to overcome these limitations and test the propositions in different geographical and industrial contexts and to operationalize the dimensions along with measuring the LIS performance from a relational perspective.

References

Ahuja, G. (2000). Collaboration networks, structural holes, and innovation: A longitudinal study. *Administrative Science Quarterly*, *45*(3), 425–455.

Balland, P. A., De Vaan, M., & Boschma, R. (2012). The dynamics of interfirm networks along the industry life cycle: The case of the global video game industry, 1987–2007. *Journal of Economic Geography*, *13*(5), 741–765.

Granovetter, M. (1985). Economic action and social structure: The problem of embeddedness. *American Journal of Sociology*, *91*(3), 481–510.

Kajikawa, Y., Takeda, Y., Sakata, I., & Matsushima, K. (2010). Multiscale analysis of interfirm networks in regional clusters. *Technovation*, *30*(3), 168–180.

Russell, M. G., Huhtamäki, J., Still, K., Rubens, N., & Basole, R. C. (2015). Relational capital for shared vision in innovation ecosystems. *Triple Helix*, *2*(1), 1–36.

Salavisa, I., Sousa, C., & Fontes, M. (2012). Topologies of innovation networks in knowledge-intensive sectors: Sectoral differences in the access to knowledge and complementary assets through formal and informal ties. *Technovation*, *32*(6), 380–399.

Saxenian, A. (1996). *Regional advantage*. Cambridge, MA: Harvard University Press.

Still, K., Huhtamäki, J., Russell, M. G., & Rubens, N. (2014). Insights for orchestrating innovation ecosystems: The case of EIT ICT Labs and data-driven network visualisations. *International Journal of Technology Management*, *66*(2–3), 243–265.

Watts, D. J., & Strogatz, S. H. (1998). Collective dynamics of "small-world" networks. *Nature*, *393*(6684), 440–442.

Index

Note: Page numbers in *italics* indicate a figure and page numbers in **bold** indicate a table.

For Product Safety Concerns and Information please contact our EU representative GPSR@taylorandfrancis.com Taylor & Francis Verlag GmbH, Kaufingerstraße 24, 80331 München, Germany

T - #0250 - 160425 - C0 - 234/156/6 - PB - 9780367730215 - Gloss Lamination